PENTAGATE

Coordinated by Thierry Meyssan

First edition

Title page photograph by: Department of Defense (DoD), *All Hands*, US Navy
Other pictures: DoD, Tech. Sgt Cedric H. Rudisill; source www.geoffmetcalf.com; US Marine Corps, Cpl. Jason Ingersoll; US Army, Sgt. Carmen L. Burgess; Jim Garamone, American Forces Press Service (see Photo section).

Library of Congress Cataloging-in-Publication Data:
Meyssan, Thierry.
The Pentagate / by Thierry Meyssan.
p.cm.
Includes bibliographical references.
ISBN 1-59209-028-1
1. American Airlines Flight 77 Hijacking Incident, 2001. 2. Terrorism — Government policy—United States
I. Title
HV6432.7.M49513 2002
975.5'295044—dc21

Carnot Publishing Ltd
20/22 Bedford Row
London WC 1R 4JS
United Kingdom

By the same author:

L'Effroyable imposture, Carnot, 2002

L'Enigma Pasqua, Golias, Paris, 2000

Charles Millon, le porte-glaive, Golias, 1999

Internet Sites :

www.reseauvoltaire.net

www.effroyable-imposture.net

www.asile.org

The book *Pentagate* and a large documentation base on 11 September and the foreign and military policies of the United States are available at: http://www.effroyable-imposture.net

DISCLAIMER

Introduction

DISSECTION OF A LIE IN WARTIME

The Big Lie strove to analyze the incoherencies of the official version of the attacks on September 11, 2001 and to present a different point of view on these events.

The French newspapers who have denigrated the book concentrated their attacks on the first chapter devoted to the strike on the Pentagon. Lacking any arguments to defend the official version, they called into question the credibility and sincerity of the author, and then the intelligence of readers.

The Big Lie contented itself with pointing out the physical impossibility of the crash of a Boeing 757 on the Pentagon without explaining the exact nature of the attack. It drew no political interpretation from the facts. In inviting citizens to a critical reading of subsequent official statements, it limited itself to underlining the fact that the government of the United States had begun to lie from the morning of 11 September.

With the help of our readers and certain of our journalist colleagues, who transmitted documents and their own reflections to us, we continued our investigations. The elements that we present today are thus not a sequel to *The Big Lie*, but a complementary study of the attack on the Pentagon and the manner in which we have been misled by the communications services of the Department of Defense.

ONE PIECE OF DEBRIS TOO MANY

A piece of debris from the Boeing 757-200 of American Airlines flight 77 was found on the lawn of the Pentagon, on 11 September 2001. Thierry Meyssan's investigation doesn't hold water. There's no longer any room for doubt: the plane did in fact crash upon the Department of Defense. Open and shut case.

But the newspapers that published the photograph of this debris as evidence may have been hasty by failing to carry out some elementary verifications. Indeed, they seem to have found a piece of debris of whose existence the Pentagon itself was unaware. It would be hard to identify, moreover, from which part of the Boeing this piece of sheet metal might come.

Debris from a "pulverized", "melted" and "gasified" airplane

The famous photograph was taken by Mark Faram, a photo-reporter for the CNA agency and initially used in *Navy Times* (see the Photo Section of this book, page XVI). It was published for the first time in France in *Le Monde* on 12 March 2002. Later, numerous other newspapers ran it full-page and in color.

This photo represents a piece of twisted sheet metal, white- and red-colored, resembling a piece of aeronautical debris. For all of the newspapers that discussed the affair, this picture meant a great deal more than that: it was photographic proof that flight AA77 had actually crashed on the Pentagon, since naturally, it represented debris from the Boeing 757-200 belonging to American Airlines.

It was *Le Monde* that set the tone in this matter. Published at the top of a page entitled, "*Internet Conveys an Extravagant Rumor About 11 September*", the photograph is captioned thusly: "*This picture was taken by a military photographer from the Navy Times, on 11 September 2001. According to the Associated Press agency which distributed it, the photo shows a piece of debris from the plane on the western heliport of the Pentagon. AP makes it clear that pieces were scattered from the point of impact all the way to the neighboring highway. It is one of the rare documents available from the photo agencies. Mark Faram, author of the snapshot, confirmed its authenticity to* Le Monde *on Monday, 19 March.*"

The editorial, published the same day, was even more categorical as to what the paper's staff thought of the picture: "*Witnesses saw the airplane before it crashed into the Pentagon, a photo even showed a piece of the fuselage a hundred meters from the building.*"[1]

At the same time, and without fear of contradiction, the newspaper reassured readers surprised by the lack of material evidence of the plane's presence: experts – anonymous ones – explained that the aircraft had disintegrated on impact and had, moreover, melted. "*The impact released an extreme energy, provoking the pulverization of the plane,*" noted one of them, "*and an immediate blaze. As opposed to cars, planes are above all composed of aluminum, which starts to liquefy towards 1,050° F and the structures of the aircraft melted.*"[2]

Later on, other newspapers took up this argument, although it was contradictory with the photo of the alleged debris. "*What about the absence of the wings? The experts in aeronautics are categorical:*

---

1. 'Internet véhicule une rumeur extravagante sur le 11 septembre' [Internet Conveys an Extravagant Rumor about 11 September], *Le Monde*, 21 March 2002.
2. 'Un avion a bel et bien frappé le Pentagone' [A Plane Really Did Hit the Pentagon], *Le Monde*, 21 March 2002 : www.lemonde.fr

composed of aluminum, they simply melted in the fire," French weekly magazine *Marianne* analyzed.[1]

Why not? But then, one should find one hundred tons of melted metal. That is not the case. To explain this mystery, one then informs readers that the temperature reached the point of gasification. "*The intensity of the heat caused by the conflagration can easily pulverize the aircraft. Meyssan does not know it perhaps, but at 5,400° F, aluminum transforms into a gas!*" *Entrevue* magazine lectured knowledgeably.[2]

Of course, no one asked themselves what would be the consequences of such a hypothesis. If the plane burned at over 5,400° F within the building, at the level of the ground and first floors, how are we to believe that the upper floors could have resisted so elevated a temperature? And how did the authorities identify the victims presumably found in this furnace? Because, as further indisputable proof of the plane crash at the Pentagon, *Libération* made clear to its readers that a passenger "*had been identified thanks to her fingerprints.*"[3]

---

1. 'Rumeurs – Le pape a-t-il organisé les attentats du 11 septembre ?' [Rumors – Did the Pope Organize the September 11 Attacks?], Eric Dior, *Marianne*, 1-7 April 2002.
2. 'Ardisson complice d'une imposture' [Ardisson an Accomplice of Fraud], *Entrevue*, April 2002.
3. 'Pourquoi la démonstration de Meyssan est cousue de très gros fils blancs' [Why Meyssan's Demonstration Is a Tissue of Lies], *Libération*, 30 March 2002.

How can we believe that metal melted, that it was "gasified", and yet the human bodies were still identifiable?

According to these newspapers, the airplane was thus "*pulverized*", before "*melting*" and being "*transformed into gas*". But they have nevertheless categorically identified a piece of debris that was not burnt at all.

The Pentagon did not find any debris

The publications that have presented this piece of debris in fact refute the official version. From the press conferences held at the Pentagon from 12 to 15 September 2001 it indeed emerges than no important piece of the airplane was found. According to the Department of Defense, the only elements that were retrieved were the black boxes and a beacon light, on 14 September 2001.

On 12 September, a journalist asked Ed Plaugher, the fire chief of Arlington county, whether anything was left of the plane. His response was unambiguous: "*First of all, the question about the aircraft, there are some small pieces of aircraft visible from the interior during this fire-fighting operation I'm talking about, but not large sections. In other words, there's no fuselage sections and that sort of thing.*"[1]

During another press conference held on 15 September, this time concerning the reconstruction of the Pentagon, Terry Mitchell was in turn questioned about what he could see as evidence of the plane. He indicated that one could only see "*small pieces*". The next question interests us in particular: "*Well, how far in?* [were these pieces of the airplane to be found?] *Again, we're trying to figure out how it came into the building ...*" The official response is eloquent: "*Can we finish the video first and then we'll go back?*" The journalists approved and of course Mr. Mitchell never went back to this question which is nevertheless primordial.[2]

Questioned also about the material evidence of the plane, Lee Evey, the head of the Pentagon renovation project, responded that there was "*considerable evidence of the aircraft outside the E ring. It's just not very visible [...] None of those parts are very large, however. You don't see big pieces of the airplane sitting there extending up into the air. But there are many small pieces. And the few larger pieces there look like they are veins out of the aircraft engine. They're circular.*"[3]

---

1. 'DoD News Briefing', Defense Link, Department of Defense, 12 September 2001:
http://www.defenselink.mil/news/Sep2001/t09122001_t0912asd.html
2. 'DoD News Briefing on Pentagon Renovation', Defense Link, Department of Defense, 15 September 2001:
http://www.defenselink.mil/news/Sep2001/t09152001_t915evey.html

On 14 September, the Department of Defense announced that the emergency workers had found the two black boxes, at four o'clock in the morning.[4] Then a beacon was found, but after that nothing more. The search was interrupted when the demolition/reconstruction work began. Of the supposed debris of the Boeing photographed by Mark Faram, there was never any mention in official statements.

In the first days following the attack, the authorities therefore mentioned only the existence of small debris, unidentifiable metallic fragments, which could have been from something quite different.

None of the firemen, architects or DoD officials saw any piece of the fuselage on the site of the attack – with the exception of the Secretary of Defense, Donald Rumsfeld (see our chapter "Disappearance of a Plane" below). Therefore the French press had six months later found a piece of the aircraft that was totally unknown to the Pentagon itself.

---

3. 'DoD News Briefing on Pentagon Renovation', op cit.
4. 'Black Boxes Found at Pentagon Crash Site', *American Forces Press Service*, Defense Link, Department of Defense, 14 September 2001:
www.defenselink.mil/news/Sep2001/n09142001_200109142.html
'Flight Data and Cockpit Voice Recorders Found', Defense Link, Department of Defense, 14 September 2001:
http://www.defenselink.mil/news/Sep2001/b09142001_bt425-01.html

Six months later, the FBI can almost reconstitute the plane

But the version of the Department of Defense is not the only official version of the story. Six months later, yet another version of the facts was offered. In April 2002, shortly after *The Big Lie* was published in France, Valérie Labrouse of the Digipresse agency returned to Washington.[1] There she contacted the authorities so that they might express their views on the subject. The statement from the FBI is troubling: its agents were said to have recovered a large part of the debris, making possible a nearly complete reconstitution of the wreck of the Boeing. This version was confirmed by Chris Murray, the FBI spokesman in Washington, when questioned by *Libération*: "*The pieces of the plane are stocked in a warehouse and they are marked with the serial numbers of flight 77.*"[2]

More than six months after the events, memory even returns to several witnesses. Ed Plaugher, the Arlington fire chief who testified in September 2001 as having only seen small pieces of the plane and not

---

1. 'Dossier 11 Septembre', *Digipresse*: http://digipressetmp4.teaser.fr/site/dossier.php?dosnum=60
2. 'Pourquoi la démonstration de Meyssan est cousue de très gros fils blancs' blancs' [Why Meyssan's Demonstration Is a Tissue of Lies], *Libération*, 30 March 2002.

"*sections*" of the fuselage, was questioned once again by Valérie Labrousse. He denied his own statements: after having recalled arriving on the scene 35 to 40 minutes after the attack, he recounts having seen "*pieces of the fuselage, the wings, the landing gear, pieces of the engine, seats. I can swear to you, it was a plane.*" Before making clear that it was an "*airliner*".[1] Thus, 35 to 40 minutes after the crash, as fires raged inside the Pentagon and with temperatures neighboring 5,400° F, high enough to burn the plane's cabin, one could approach the inferno and make out seats from the Boeing. Ed Plaugher even indicates having "*seen*" (sic) one of the two black boxes, that nevertheless would not be found until three days later. A black box that is officially unusable because it was left exposed too long to extreme heat.

Libération published another testimony on 30 March 2002, confirming the presence of debris. According to Arthur Santana, "*emergency workers collected pieces of the plane all over the place. The pieces were put in brown plastic bags that were marked with the letters "evidence" and part of this zone was surrounded by yellow tape. A big piece of the plane, lifted by two persons, allowed you to clearly see the letter "C" of American Airlines.*"[2]

---

1. 'Ed Plaugher: La mémoire à rebours' [Ed Plaugher : Memory in Reverse] *Digipresse*, 22 May 2002 :
http://digipressetmp4.teaser.fr/site/page.php?numart=487&doss=60

The Parisian daily also published another account, that of Mike Walter: "*After the explosion, I walked in the direction of the Pentagon. I was more than a hundred yards from the impact, but there were pieces of fuselage all over. Several times I had to step over the debris. I even remember someone picking up a piece and having their picture taken, with the Pentagon in the background.*" According to *Libération*, "*the journalist nevertheless confirms the debris of the plane was not in large-sized pieces.*" On 11 April, Jamie McIntyre, CNN correspondent at the Pentagon, confided to *Paris-Match* the manner in which he experienced the crash, which occurred while he was in his office at the Pentagon. "*I immediately ran towards the scene of the crash. Hundreds of pieces of plane littered the ground, including a piece of the fuselage and a part of the cockpit window that CNN had analyzed by experts.*"[3]

We're now being told of imposing pieces of debris that are identifiable and even of photos taken of these pieces. However, none of these pictures (with the exception of Mark Faram's) have been

---

2. 'Pourquoi la démonstration de Meyssan est cousue de très gros fils blancs' blancs' [Why Meyssan's Demonstration Is a Tissue of Lies], op cit.

3. 'Pentagone, la rumeur pulvérisée' [Pentagon: The Rumor Pulverized], Saveria Rojek and Romain Clergeat, *Paris-Match*, 11 April 2002.

published, or even preserved by the press agencies. Why? And how is it that the Pentagon, which only found, officially, a beacon and two black boxes, was unaware of all this debris from the Boeing on its own lawn?

Without calling into question the reliability of this new testimony, at the very least it raises the question of its interpretation.

A problematical photo

The argument that allows this unidentified fragment of debris to be made into a piece of the fuselage is the resemblance of its colors. In effect, it seems that the red bordered by white corresponds with the colors of American Airlines. However, the first troubling detail is that the piece of debris does not seem to have the characteristic silvery color of the American company's planes. Furthermore, upon examining closely photographs available of the Boeing 757-200's owned by this company, it appears difficult to identify any spot from which this piece of fuselage might have come from.

The curved bend of red and white excludes it from being part of the very angular letters "AA" that are featured on the tail. In the same way, a study of the wide red, white and blue band that runs around the cabin and also figures on the plane's nose allows one to assert that the piece of debris does not come from there. The wings have no red at all, but only black and white. The underbelly of the aircraft is solely of a metallic gray color. There thus remains only the word “American” inscribed on the side of the Boeing. But again there is a problem: the shape of the colors seems to indicate that it belongs to the corner of a letter. And therefore one should see, just to the side, the border of the letter that follows. However, one is unable to make out any such thing in the photo. There is the possibility that it’s from the last letter of the word. But there, we have yet another problem: one should be able to see the outline of the door, adjacent to the letter “n”. Nothing like that appears in the photo.

The piece of debris having been deformed by the explosion, it seems nevertheless dubious to assert that it absolutely could not come from a Boeing owned by American Airlines. But it’s just as dubious to affirm that it is necessarily part of the cabin; nothing is less certain and no piece seems correspond with it. As for the colors that we are told are necessarily those of American Airlines, they are above all those of the United States. One therefore finds them on a great number of official or military vehicles and aircraft.

One recalls that, according to numerous witnesses, a helicopter was parked in front of the façade, just before the explosion. Some of them say that the aircraft that struck the Pentagon first hit the helicopter before embedding itself in the façade.[1] Why couldn't this piece of debris have come from that helicopter?

"It's not evidence, but it's presented as if it were"

The Pentagon itself declared in September 2001 that no important pieces existed. There is thus little chance that this famous fragment of debris comes from flight AA77. Hervé Kempf, a journalist for *Le Monde*, could not be unaware of all these inconsistencies. On 23 March 2002, during the television program + *Clair* aired by the French TV station Canal +, Thierry Meyssan confronted him with the contradictions raised by the publication of this photo in the Parisian evening paper.

Thierry Meyssan: "*This is a very interesting falsification. The newspaper* Le Monde, *seeking to mislead its readers, has published a photograph originating from an official photographer of the navy of the United States.*"

Daphné Roulier, presenter of the program [in English]: "*US Navy*"

---

1. See notably: 'Blessés, incendies et débris au Pentagone" [Wounded, Fires and Debris at the Pentagon], *Agence France-Presse*, 11 September 2001. Article reproduced by *Cyberpresse*:
http://www.cyberpresse.ca/reseau/monde/0109/mon_101090013337.html

Thierry Meyssan: "*In this photograph, one sees a piece of metal that is not identifiable.* [...] *The Department of Defense told us that only the plane's beacon was found on the lawn. Thus, according to the authorities, this is not an element of the plane. Yet the newspaper* Le Monde [...] *uses this as an argument.* [It] *pretends to be ignorant of the press conference held on 15 September that we* [Thierry Meyssan and Hervé Kempf] *discussed at length. And you questioned me several times about this photograph. But to lend further credibility to it, they indicate that they contacted the author of the photograph to assure themselves of its authenticity – about which no one doubts, but which says strictly nothing as to the significance of the picture.* [...] *I would like to know why the newspaper* Le Monde *tried to mislead its readers with this photo.* [...]"

Hervé Kempf: "*Well now! It's very interesting that Thierry Meyssan cites this photo and what he says about it is true. That is to say, I agree with him and there was a debate over it among the editorial staff at* Le Monde – *because the editorial staff there is not a monolithic bloc. And personally, along with other journalists, I was opposed to the publication of this photo that was presented as evidence. You are perfectly right to point out that it isn't evidence and it's presented as if it were:* 'Ah! You see now that Mr. Meyssan is wrong because here is a piece of debris from the plane!' *If one reads the caption attentively, however, one sees that there is no ambiguity.*"

One can indeed reread the caption of the photograph, quoted above, and agree with Mr. Kempf: there is no ambiguity, this piece of debris is presented as part of the Boeing's wreckage, even if the paternity of this authentication is attributed to Associated Press. As for the editorial, it was totally affirmative. For the record, let's quote the Associated Press's own caption: "*A piece of the plane wreck lies next to the heliport on the west side of the Pentagon, after a terrorist attack on Tuesday, 11 September 2001 in Arlington, Virginia. Debris from the plane was spread beyond the expressway and military medical teams were mobilizing to bring first aid to the wounded.*"

What, then, has Hervé Kempf just told us? That he knew that this photograph did not represent "*evidence*". That he said as much during a meeting of the editorial staff. But since "*an editorial staff is not some monolithic bloc*", the other journalists, who formed a majority or were higher up in the hierarchy, nevertheless chose to publish this photo without any guarantee as to what it might represent. And its publication is even accompanied by a caption and an editorial that aim to leave the reader in no doubt as to the nature of the debris, that of course it comes from American Airlines' missing Boeing 757-200. Now that is an interesting conception of the reliability of information within a newspaper.

Hervé Kempf's televised declaration is very hard on the newspaper he works for. We questioned the journalist in order to allow him to express himself further and go back over this episode. He thinks the photo does in fact represent a piece of the Boeing, but also confirmed that he was opposed to its publication: "*I had a problem with the utilization of the photo as proof. For me, what counts is the context, the author, the conditions in which the document is produced, the sociological environment of this production.* [...] *Well, at that time, we hadn't been able to question Mark Faram. We had contacted him by e-mail and he had merely confirmed being the author of the photo.*" Kempf develops his methodological conception of investigative reporting: "*For me, the essential thing is the testimony. I'm trained as a historian, and in history, testimony is primordial.*" We will see later that the analysis of various testimonies also should have resulted in greater caution. In the meantime, it does seem that *Le Monde* showed reprehensible haste: they published a photo of debris without taking any methodological precautions, without even having talked about it with the author, and without taking into account the contradictions that this document raises in relation with the Pentagon's official version. We have here a lack of rigor on the part of *Le Monde*, all the more surprising because the newspaper's editorial piece devoted itself to preaching lessons in professional ethics to Thierry Meyssan.

Convince the reader at any cost?

On the evening of 23 March 2002 when the Canal + program was broadcast, the French public thus learned that the photograph of debris published in *Le Monde* did not constitute "*evidence*". It also learned that this piece of debris was not included among the elements officially recovered by the American military. Its authenticity, insofar as being debris from the Boeing, was thus in serious doubt.

And yet, in the days following the broadcast, numerous publications would, without fearing to lead their readers astray, continue to reproduce this photograph as evidence against Thierry Meyssan's investigation. Successively, *Marianne*[1], *Entrevue*[2] and *Paris-Match*[3] would all publish Mark Faram's photo again, without the slightest rhetorical precaution.

For Saveria Rojek, a journalist for *Paris-Match* who works in the United States, Hervé Kempf's contribution on Canal + did not constitute

---

1. 'Rumeurs – Le pape a-t-il organisé les attentats du 11 septembre ?' [Rumors – Did the Pope Organize the September 11 Attacks?], Eric Dior, *Marianne*, 1-7 April 2002.
2. 'Ardisson complice d'une imposture' [Ardisson an Accomplice of Fraud], *Entrevue*, April 2002.
3. 'Pentagone, la rumeur pulvérisée' [Pentagon: The Rumor Pulverized], Saveria Rojek and Romain Clergeat, *Paris-Match*, 11 April 2002.

sufficient motive to block publication of the photo. This journalist, as a matter of fact, had the nature of the debris "*authenticated*" by an expert. According to the latter, the color green that he discerned on the internal part of the debris was characteristic of the paint used in the aeronautics industry to protect the cabin from corrosion and this proved that we had here a fragment of debris from American Airlines flight 77. Saveria Rojek also received the opinion of the photographer, Mark Faram: "*I arrived at the scene four minutes after the crash because I was having breakfast in the Pentagon building. The place looked like a plane crash site. I was in the Navy during the 1970's and was assigned to emergency rescue operations, including airplane disasters. I've seen plenty of crash scenes. When I saw this piece lying on the ground, I had no doubt: it was a piece of an airplane. That silver color, those blue and red stripes, it was undeniably an American Airlines plane. It was the biggest piece that I saw. It was absolutely impossible that someone could have brought it to this spot because there was practically nobody there at that time. Other smaller pieces were scattered all around, silvery aluminum-colored and green on the inside.*" The authentication by the expert and the photographer's testimony thus permitted the journalist to publish the photo "*whatever the case may be*".

However, numerous questions remain unanswered. For example, since this type of paint is also used for helicopter cabins, how does its presence permit one to affirm that it had to be debris from a Boeing 757-200? From which part of the plane does it come from? Why did the American authorities not recover it? Why was there no other visible debris? Was it because the plane had disintegrated, melted and been gasified? We've received no answers to any of these questions.

In an inset to the same article, *Paris-Match* also published a second piece of "*evidence*". In a pile of unidentifiable materials, one can barely distinguish a dark, circular form, vaguely resembling a tire. In view of the poor quality of the photo, one wonders if it's not one of those psychological tests where each subject is invited to project his or her own fantasy. Yet *Paris-Match* affirms that it has reproduced there, "*dislocated, but perfectly identifiable (sic), a tire from the landing gear*", that had also "*been found*". This tire was found by whom? Shouldn't the happy owner of this cumbersome object have sent it to the American authorities, who in September possessed only a beacon and black boxes? There again, no answer...

The "counter-investigation" on Internet

The same haste characterizes all of the newspapers that published this photo of debris presenting it without any reservations as belonging to the Boeing 757-200 of American Airlines. Most of the journalists did not even carry out the minimal checking that Saveria Rojek did in gathering the opinion of the photographer and an expert. The counter-investigative effort was finally reduced to very little indeed. In their desire to counter a "*rumor coming from the Net*" many newspapers thought it useful to send readers to two Internet sites presented as the ultimate references: the French-language Hoaxbuster[1] and the English-speaking Snopes.[2] The work of counter-investigation does not, however, seem to have carried out any better by these sites.

Snopes, for example, as opposed to the official version, affirms that "*all five rings*" were damaged by the Boeing. To support this assertion, the site published a photo of the Pentagon undergoing rebuilding work, taken on... 11 March 2002, six months after the events, and above all, after the authorities had demolished the entire wing for reconstruction.

---

1. http://www.hoaxbuster.com/hdossier/pentagone/pentagone.html (the English expression "hoax buster", modelled on the title of the famous film *Ghostbusters*, designates someone who "expels rumors".

2. http://www.snopes2.com/rumors/pentagon.htm

According to the authors of these pages, this proves beyond the shadow of a doubt that the plane caused considerably more damage than that described in *The Big Lie*. But since, apparently, the contradiction doesn't bother them, a few lines later they make it clear that – only – three of the five rings were damaged by the plane. Faced with such a presentation of the facts, it is no longer eventual proof of the plane's existence that one is looking for, but rather some sign of sincerity from the site's authors.

Again contradicting itself, Snopes indicates a little later in its text that, "*according to what witnesses describe and what the photos show*", the plane hit the ground before impact, which considerably reduced its speed and thus the damage it could cause. To our knowledge, no witness has related such a version. Besides which, the various photographs officially released on the American army's sites show that the lawn was perfectly intact. Snopes does not in fact cite any testimony on this point, nor has it published the photos to which it refers...

In order to explain the disappearance of the wings, the two sites give the same response: they were folded back against the cabin, and then penetrated inside the building with rest of the plane, before finally burning or melting. "*It's highly probable that they were folded back along the cabin at the moment of impact*", Hoaxbuster explains with great seriousness. "*As the front of the Boeing 757 hit the Pentagon, the outer portions of the wings likely snapped during the initial impact, then were pushed inward towards the fuselage and carried into the building's interior; the inner portions of the wings probably penetrated the Pentagon walls with the rest of the plane.*"

This highly "original" explanation does not permit us to understand the lack of any impact by the wings against the façade. One does not see very well how the impact of the plane's nose could have caused the wings to retract. It's nonsense in physical terms: with the kinetic energy, the broken portions of the wings would have been propelled forwards rather than backwards along the fuselage, and would have struck the façade with their leading edges like a whiplash. In passing, the authors' reasoning forgets that the jet engines – two of the most resistant parts of the airplane – are fixed to these same wings and would have necessarily "marked" the façade.

Lastly, to explain the fact that this Boeing could have escaped the fighter jets sent in its pursuit, Hoaxbuster launches into a most curious explanation: "*Flight AA77 crashed into the Pentagon at 9:43 am. The American fighters took off at 10 am (that is, more than a half hour after the crash) and contented themselves with following flight 93 that ended its journey in Shanksville, Pennsylvania. And if they had chased after the* [Pentagon] *plane, they would not have shot it down over an urban area (this would have the effect of producing many more victims).*" One does not know the provenance of these suppositions. All the more so as NORAD has, on the contrary, officially let it be known that two F-16's took off at 9:30 am (see Appendices), that is, six minutes after being notified of the hijacking by the FAA and thirty-five minutes after the aircraft's transponder was cut off.[1] Thus, in trying to fly to the rescue of the official version, Hoaxbuster contradicts it.

How does one explain the excessive esteem that journalists have for these two sites, which are manifestly unfit for this type of work? The people writing for Hoaxbuster themselves recognize that, "*we're not experts in aeronautics, or in plane crashes, or in explosives*". Paradoxically, after having attempted to discredit an investigative book by calling it "*rumor by Internet*", some newspapers had no problems about seeking recourse, with considerable complacency, in Internet sites that are relatively incompetent on such technical terrain...

Also, why have these newspapers cited so many – anonymous – experts, at times contradicting their own statements about the existence of debris from the plane? Why haven't they cited François Grangier, an expert accident investigator, who is

---

1. 'NORAD's Response Times' : chronology distributed to the press on 15 September 2001 by the North American Aerospace Defense Command (NORAD). See document in Appendices.

usually invited by the French media to comment on air catastrophes? Is it because he recognized publicly that the Boeing in no case could have struck the facade? "*What is certain when one looks at the photo of this façade that remains intact is that it's obvious the plane did not go through there. It's like imagining that a plane of this size could pass through a window and leave the frame still standing. But it's obvious that if there was a plane, it must have hit somewhere else*".[1]

Looking to defend the official version, the authors of *L'Effroyable mensonge* [The Horrendous Lie] questioned François Grangier. Unfortunately, the latter confirmed his analysis: "*I think the trajectory as far as one can make it out today rules out an impact against the façade, but more likely one upon the roof.*"[2] All of the official declarations and photographic images, whether they come from the American army or press agencies show without any ambiguity that the aircraft did not strike the roof but the façade (see the Photo Section of this book).

So why don't the partisans of the official thesis seem more disturbed by this manifest contradiction or even pay any notice to it?

---

1. + *Clair* (television news program), Canal +, 23 March 2002.
2. *L'Effroyable mensonge* [The Horrendous Lie], Guillaume Dasquié and Jean Guisnel, ed. La Découverte, June 2002, pp. 43-44.

TRUNCATED TESTIMONIES

The testimonies cited by the French press are unanimous: all the witnesses – "thousands of people"[1] according to some – saw a Boeing 757-200 belonging to the American Airlines company strike the façade of the Pentagon and disappear into the building. Yet a rigorous analysis of the content of their testimonies imposes, there again, greater caution. The accounts published in Paris, six months after the events, differ sometimes widely from the original testimonies gathered "on the spot" across the Atlantic. The elements contradicting the official version have even been hidden altogether.

---

1. *L'Effroyable mensonge* [The Horrible Lie], Guillaume Dasquié and Jean Guisnel, ed. La Découverte, June 2002 (text on back cover). See also page 56 : "thousands of American citizens saw the crash of the Boeing".

Contradictory first testimonies

The first testimonies to be gathered and published were in an article that appeared in the *Washington Post* dated Tuesday, 11 September 2001, at 4:59 pm.[1] Because it was the first sampling of witnesses, its value as a document is precious. The testimonies are less likely to be the object of a real reconstruction, because the media steamroller had barely been set in motion.

What then, do these four witnesses of the initial moments have to tell us? First of all, there is Kirk Milburn, building site director for Atlantis Co. He speaks of an airplane, of debris flying in the air. Not of a Boeing. "*I heard a plane. I saw it. I saw debris fly in the air. I imagine that it hit the lampposts. It went 'Whoosh, whoosh', then there was fire and smoke, and I heard a second explosion.*" His auditory memory is precise: the aircraft made a peculiar sound and there were two distinct explosions.

The second witness quoted is Steve Patterson, a graphics expert aged forty-three who saw a silvery vehicle pass in front of the window of his apartment, on the 14th floor of a building in Pentagon City. The

---

1. 'Extensive Casualities in Wake of Pentagon Attack', *Washington Post*, 11 September 2001, 4:59 pm (forty-eight journalists contributed to this article): www.washingtonpost.com

Washington Post reports his testimony in these terms: "*The plane, which made a shrill noise like a fighter plane, flew over Arlington cemetery, so low that he thought it was going to land on I-395*." He also said that the plane flew so fast that he could not read what was inscribed on its fuselage. But his description of the object is nevertheless precise: "*The airplane, which seemed to be able to hold eight or twelve persons, went straight towards the Pentagon*." A graphics expert by profession, this witness was relatively far away from the Pentagon, while at a reasonable distance from the aircraft, which allowed him to see it for a long while; his testimony is precise and clearly conflicts with the official version. It is all the more surprising because it does not correspond with the frame of mind in which he found himself at the moment of these events; since he was watching pictures on television of a Boeing crashing into the World Trade Center, this could have influenced him. It is thus not simply a mental construct after the fact, as many of the testimonies emanating from people who were too close to the Pentagon manifestly are. Their time of observation lasted less than a second with a reduced field of vision. What he says contradicts the official thesis: indeed, he does not speak of a Boeing but of a small plane for 8 to 12 passengers, producing the noise of a jet fighter.

Unfortunately, Thierry Meyssan and his team have not succeeded in questioning him in the course of their investigation. Very probably, this awkward witness no longer wishes to respond to questions by the press. He has been impossible to get hold of... except for *Paris-Match*, one of whose correspondents, Romain Clergeat, succeeded in tracking down Steve Patterson and getting him to speak.

Here are the remarks that the Paris weekly indicates it gathered directly: "*I was watching the pictures of the World Trade Center when I saw a plane pass before my window flying so low that one had the impression that it was seeking to land on the I-395 highway, but so fast that I couldn't read what was on the fuselage. Then I saw it heading towards the Pentagon lower than the tops of tree and crash into it. The plane was absorbed by the building and an enormous ball of fire then emerged.*" In this new account, which takes up almost word for word the initial testimony that appeared in the *Washington Post*, two phrases have disappeared: they are "*that seemed able to carry 8 to 12 persons*" and the reference to the "*shrill sound of a fighter plane*".

We questioned the American bureau of *Paris-Match*. Saveria Rojek affirmed that Steve Patterson's comments had been gathered personally by her colleague Romain Clergeat and that she was unable to explain the variations in this testimony. She couldn't remember how Steve Patterson had been located and was sorry for having mislaid, since then, his address and telephone number. Too bad...

Patterson's name was also mentioned by *Libération*[1] and *Le Monde*[2] as that of a witness "against" Thierry Meyssan, without at any moment pointing out the fundamental divergence between his account and the official version.

Let's continue with the four witnesses who testified in the first hours following the attack. The third, Asework Hagos, who was driving on Columbia Pike, said he saw an airplane flying extremely low, close to the surrounding buildings. He also indicates he recognized the American Airlines insignia, before seeing the aircraft crash into the Pentagon. And Tom Seibert, a systems engineer who works at the Pentagon, is the last witness on this first list. He said: "*We heard something that made the sound of a missile, then we heard a powerful boom.*"

The others quoted in this article were only indirect witnesses of the attack. We thus dispose of four principal testimonies collected on 11 September by the *Washington Post*. The first, Kirk Milburn, does not speak of a Boeing but of a "*plane*" making a peculiar noise. The second, Steve Patterson, speaks of small plane capable of containing between eight and twelve persons, and making a shrill noise like a

---

1. 'Pourquoi la démonstration de Meyssan est cousue de très gros fils blancs' blancs' [Why Meyssan's Demonstration Is a Tissue of Lies], *Libération*, 30 March 2002.
2. 'Un avion a bel et bien frappé le Pentagone' [A Plane Really Did Hit the Pentagon], *Le Monde*, 21 March 2002 : www.lemonde.fr

fighter aircraft. The third, Asework Hagos, identifies an American Airlines aircraft. Finally, the last witness, Tom Seibert, did not see the aircraft, but heard the sound of a missile.

It's difficult to form a definite opinion on the subject solely by reading these testimonies. Before going any further, it's advisable to recall certain principles about gathering testimony in the case of traumatic scenes, and to describe the phenomenon of feedback.

Reminders on the debriefing of witnesses

Gathering testimony is a difficult exercise. Any interview situation, in a general way, involves biases that will modify the nature of the words recorded.

First of all, a witness unconsciously has a tendency to adapt his comments to his listener, and to propose to him the version that seems most likely to enhance his or her standing.

Secondly, when it's a question of events of social or political significance, a witness will tend to align him or herself with the implicated social group of which he or she feels representative. For example, let us imagine a traffic accident involving a car driver, a cyclist and a pedestrian. The "driver" witnesses will have a tendency to accuse the cyclist or the pedestrian, while the "cyclist witnesses will have a tendency to exonerate the cyclist, and the "pedestrian" witnesses to exonerate the pedestrian.

Consciously or not, voluntarily or not, witnesses always have a propensity to construct a version of events that corresponds with their social role.

This behavior, which can be observed in any interview, for example those carried out in the course of a sociological or psychological study, is particularly interesting when it applies to a traumatic incident, especially if the latter occurred rapidly or in a confusing fashion. Indeed, in this type of situation, the individual's various sensory organs often lack the possibility of capturing the event in a complete manner, and it's then the brain that will combine the different elements perceived to construct an intellectually coherent version. This phenomenon is known as "feedback". It's a reflex that consists in instinctively replacing a sensation that has been poorly identified by the sensory organ with another that belongs to acquired memory. Thus, when one hears a sound or a group of sounds poorly, the psycho-auditory zone replaces it by substituting another sound that it knows. The same applies to vision. An image that is too fleeting to be seen distinctly is replaced by another the mind has already encountered before and which belongs to the acquired visual memory. To do this, the brain will associate the different sensorial elements (sound, fleeting image, environment...) to deduce in a fraction of a second what it has "seen". But this association can also be the source of error: one can cite the example of a weapons engineer who had never seen a military drone. When he saw one pass by him at high speed he made a mistake and identified it with precision as a Mirage 2000, and yet the latter was an aircraft that he knew well and whose presence in that vicinity was very unlikely.

Let's imagine for an instant an aircraft with silver, red and white colors, flying at low altitude and high speed, with a shrill sound, in an urban area. What is the likelihood that those witnessing the aircraft's passage, not having time to identify it, will reconstruct *a posteriori*, through a feedback reflex, the familiar image of a Boeing? It's difficult to evaluate, but the probability is high.

Witnesses who saw too much

In most situations, investigators gather conflicting testimonies whose reliability they must evaluate, case by case.

Concerning the attack on the Pentagon, let's take the example of Steve Riskus, a witness abundantly quoted by the press. Like many people, he was on the highway that runs past the Pentagon. According to his statement, the cars on that road had almost come to a halt due to a traffic jam. He was nevertheless in the middle of driving, paying more attention to the road than to the skies. He also made it clear to Digipresse that he was listening to the news on the radio about the World Trade Center at the very moment when a Boeing appeared suddenly before his very eyes.[1] According to the reconstitution carried out by Valérie Labrousse at the scene, the aircraft crossed Steve Riskus's field of vision in less than two seconds. It was about one hundred yards in front of him, moving at close to 310 miles per hour. It is thus physically impossible that he could have observed in that instant the details he describes today in his testimony: "*I was driving on Highway 27, with the Pentagon on my left. The plane came in from the right, very low, hitting one or two lampposts. I was so afraid that I ducked my head inside the car. It was so close I could clearly see the red and blue of the American Airlines cabin.*" It's a little as if he had seen a French high-speed train pass before his eyes, and was able to spot the location of the bar-wagon, while ducking his head.

Let's take another witness, quoted in *Le Monde*, to whom Hervé Kempf told us he attached considerable credit. This was David Winslow, an Associated Press reporter, living in a ten floor building close to the Pentagon. Here is his testimony, as it was published in *Le Monde*: "*I was off work that*

---

1. 'Steve Riskus : comme un dessin animé' [Steve Riskus: Like a Cartoon], *Digipresse*, 22 May 2002.

day. I was watching pictures on television of the attacks on New York. At that moment, towards 9:30 am, I heard an enormous sound of airplane engines – my brother is a pilot, as is a good friend of mine, so I know this sound[1] *–, I heard it become louder and louder, and I turned my head to the right. Through the window I saw the enormous tail of a plane passing at full speed. I could distinguish a red logo. And then bang on the Pentagon, an enormous ball of fire. I've been a journalist for many years, and I would swear it on my life: it was a plane.*" Why did Hervé Kempf place such value in this testimony, whose interest is quite limited? He gave us three reasons: "*Firstly, he was a general affairs journalist at Associated Press, where accuracy is a religion. Secondly, he does not work on military affairs. Thirdly, he has personal experience around airplanes.*" And then he added: "*He was looking at the pictures of the World Trade Center, so he was psychologically ready to see what he was going to see.*"

There is the whole problem.

---

1. Without other comments on our part, this point surprised us: do you need a brother who's a pilot to recognize the sound of an airplane?

Explosive metaphors...

Two other witnesses, Mike Walter and Joel Sucherman, say more than they'd like to think. Both of them work for the national daily, *USA Today*, but were witnesses separately of the attack. Both have recourse, however, to the same metaphor: this plane did not behave like a plane, but like a missile.

Joel Sucherman, first of all, said that from his car he saw the plane go by less than 75 yards in front of him, before it crashed 100 yards further on, into the Pentagon. If one estimates, as the official version would have it, that the plane was flying at over 300 knots (at least 315 mph), it would have traveled this distance in a maximum of 0.75 seconds. A little short, perhaps, to perceive "*a silver airplane with the distinctive marks along the windows that made say that was an American Airlines plane.*" And then he adds, concerning the plane's trajectory: "*But whoever was flying the plane made no attempt to change direction. It was coming in at a high rate of speed, but not at a steep angle – almost like a heat-seeking missile was locked on its target and staying dead on course.*"[1]

---

1. 'Journalist Witnesses Pentagon Crash', *eWeek*, 13 September 2001:
http://www.eweek.com/article/0,3658,s%253D704%2526a%253D15161,00.asp

Mike Walter was also on the highway, with rush-hour traffic almost at a standstill. Looking through his window, he saw coming "*a plane, a plane from American Airlines. I thought:* 'That's not right, it's really low'. *And I saw it. I mean, it was like a cruise missile with wings.*"[1] Questioned by Digipresse in March 2002, Mike Walter indicated that he had spoken metaphorically.[2] We never doubted him on that point. But the choice of this metaphor remains striking. All the more so because for him, it was a question of principle: it could not be a missile, because he "*couldn't imagine the possibility of a plot or any responsibility whatsoever on the part of the military leaders or the American government in the attacks of 11 September.*"

After his first declaration to CNN, Mike Walter would offer two new versions of the arrival of the plane at the Pentagon. On 21 March 2002, appearing on the French cable TV news, *LCI*, he claimed that the plane "*folded like an accordion*" against the façade. A few days later, he affirmed to Digipresse that the Boeing "*continued its trajectory inside the Pentagon, but its wings didn't enter the building*". According

1. 'Up to 800 Possibly Dead at Pentagon', *CNN*, 12 September 2001: http://www.cnn.com/2001/US/09/11/pentagon.terrorism/
2. 'Mike Walter: "Ni missile, ni bombe, un avion American Airlines"' [Mike Walter: "Neither a Missile, Not a Bomb, but American Airlines Plane], *Digipresse*, 22 May 2002 : http://digipressetmp4.teaser.fr/site/page.php?numart=492&doss=60

to this journalist, they were "*folded back*". The aircraft was also said to have "*disintegrated*". He was nevertheless able to see numerous pieces of debris (see his interview in the Appendices).

These declarations are intriguing in relation to the other testimonies gathered. Mike Walter is indeed the only person to describe the instant when the vehicle hit the façade. Other witnesses spoke distinctly of two events: on the one hand, the aircraft that they see or hear, and on the other, the explosion.

A peculiar sound and trajectory

If numerous witnesses have related having seen a Boeing from American Airlines, a number of them nevertheless describe a trajectory and a sound that cannot be those of such an aircraft.

Thus, many state having heard a shrill sound: Omar Campo, who was mowing grass on the other side of the highway, speaks of an American Airlines jetliner, that "*came in screaming over my head*".[1] One recalls Patterson speaking of plane making "*a shrill sound like a fighter plane*" and Tom Seibert evoking "*the sound of a missile*". Joel Sucherman also speaks of a shrill sound, as does Afework Hagos.

1. 'Everyone was screaming, crying, running. It's like a war zone', *The Guardian*, 12 September 2001:
http://www.guardian.co.uk/Print/0,3858,4254882,00.html

James Ryan, 27 years old, has an even more precise version, and notes an interesting detail: as the plane passed over him, he heard "*a strange sound that he interpreted as being the sudden cut-out of the engines. He therefore raised his eyes and gazed at an aircraft flying at very low altitude that he identified immediately, he said, as being an American Airlines Boeing. He makes clear that he saw the company's logo, that the aircraft was silver in color and he also affirms that he could make out the windows. The plane flew over his car. At that instant he saw it waggle its wings as if it were gliding and that it had just 'missed the radio tower' in trying to stabilize. Then, with a shrill sound, the plane accelerated and sped straight ahead in the direction of the west wing of the Pentagon.*"[1]

The waggling of the wings was confirmed by numerous witnesses, although the explanations varied: Afework Hagos thus said that "*plane was tilting its wings up and down, like it was trying to balance*".[2] Aydan Kizildrgli noted that the plane "*banked slightly*" before impact.[3] Mark Bright, a security agent at the Pentagon, heard, like James Ryan, a "*throttle-up*" just before the plane hit the building.[4]

We've asked for opinions from pilots of Boeing 767's or 777's. For all of them, the behavior described by the witnesses was strange. For example, it is possible for a Boeing to oscillate on the axis of its wings, in order to adjust a trajectory. But it's impossible for this oscillation to be very rapid, as the Boeing 757 is a massive machine. To waggle its wings up and down, in the rapid movement evoked by Afework Hagos, is difficult to envisage. In the same way, while it's possible to throttle down the engines sharply, before throttling up again to full power, and thus give the illusion having cut off the engines then accelerated, this maneuver takes at least ten seconds for a Boeing. A length of time that James Ryan did not dispose of... In all cases, these testimonies concerning the sound and the trajectory also correspond perfectly with the manner in which a missile flies in the final phase of flight, just before it strikes its target.

* * *

---

1. 'James Ryan : "C'était un cauchemar"' [James Ryan: "It Was a Nightmare", *Digipresse*, 22 Mai 2002:
http://digipressetmp4.teaser.fr/site/page.php?num_art=488&doss=60
2. 'Everyone was screaming, crying, running. It's like a war zone', *The Guardian*, 12 September 2001, op cit.
3. 'Bush vows retaliation for "evil acts"', *USA Today*, 12 September 2001:
http://www.usatoday.com/news/nation/2001/09/11/attack-usat.htm
4. 'The Pentagon's first heroes in a day of heroes', *DCMilitary*, 28 September 2001:
http://www.dcmilitary.com/marines/hendersonhall/6_39/local_news/10797-1.html

The study of the testimonies and their contradictions permits us to conclude that the attack did indeed involve a flying vehicle with propulsion engines. It thus allows us to discard the hypotheses of a booby-trapped vehicle or a helicopter. The nature of the aircraft that struck the Pentagon remains, however, very problematical. The witnesses do not allow us in fact to determine whether it was a plane or a missile, and still less to affirm that it was American Airlines flight 77. We now need to confront the missile hypothesis with the material evidence.

THE MISSILE HYPOTHESIS

Immediately after the attack on the Pentagon, the *New York Times* reported on the extent of the damage: the aircraft "*crashed into the outer edge of the building between the first and second floors,* 'at full power' *Mr. Rumsfeld said. It penetrated three of the five concentric rings of the building.*"[1] One in fact observes in the photographs distributed mainly by the army that the vehicle pierced a hole measuring several yards wide in the façade. It penetrated the building without touching the ground, which is totally intact. It came out again, three buildings further, creating a perfectly round hole about seven feet in diameter.

What kind of vehicle could have caused this damage: a Boeing 757-200 or a missile?

---

1. 'A Hijacked Boeing 757 Slams into the Pentagon', *New York Times*, 12 September 2001:
http://www.americanmemorials.com/memorial/tribute.asp?idMemorial=1316&idContributor=7466

The impact

The machine crashed into the west façade of the Pentagon, in front of which lies the heliport. Half an hour after the attack, about sixty feet of this façade had collapsed. A fire propagated itself throughout the entire wing of the building, causing enormous destruction. The biggest damages, however, were caused by the water utilized to extinguish the fire, as was made clear by fire chief Ed Plaugher[1], and also by the head of the building's renovation project, Lee Evey.[2] Later, the decision would be taken to raze the whole wing, nearly 300 feet, in order to reconstruct anew.

The impact itself is nevertheless quite narrow. The photograph on page VI of the color Photo Section of this book was taken in the very first minutes, upon the arrival of rescue teams, by Corporal James Ingersoll of the United States Marines. In it, one can observe the façade which has not yet collapsed and the point of the aircraft's impact. The orifice was magnified in the next picture. It extends from the ground level to the first floor of the building (about 25 feet high). Its width corresponds to that of two

---

1. 'DoD News Briefing', Defense Link, Department of Defense, 12 September 2001:
http://www.defenselink.mil/news/Sep2001/t09122001_t0912asd.html
2. 'DoD News Briefing on Pentagon Renovation', Defense Link, Department of Defense, 15 September 2001:
http://www.defenselink.mil/news/Sep2001/t09152001_t915evey.html

windows above (about 17 to 20 feet wide). It seems, however, that the external wall was carried off between the two supporting pillars, and that the hole was thus larger that the vehicle which crashed into it.

The aircraft that passed through this orifice thus measured less than 17 to 20 feet in diameter. That could correspond to the passenger cabin of a Boeing 757-200 which in fact measures 11.5 feet. But this plane also possesses wings that give a total breadth of 125 feet. Fixed upon these wings are the jet engines that constitute two of the aircraft's most solid elements. Finally, the plane also has a big tail. When the landing gear is not deployed, the Boeing measures a little more than 40 feet high. In this picture one can see that the wall just above the hole is still intact. It was thus not hit by the tail of a Boeing 757-200.

The exit hole

The photograph on page XII (which also appears on the front cover) was provided by the Department of Defense. It shows the hole from which the aircraft emerged. The picture's initial caption, published on a Navy Web site, indicates: "*the exit hole where American Airlines Flight 77 finally stopped after penetrating the Pentagon.*"[1] This hole is perfectly round and measures about seven feet wide.

---

1. 'War and Readiness', *All Hands*, magazine of the US Navy: http://www.mediacen.navy.mil/pubs/allhands/nov01/pg16.htm

The two pictures and their blow-ups on pages XIV and XV show the emplacement of the hole. It is located in the inner façade of the third ring. The aircraft penetrated three buildings at an angle of about 45° to the perpendicular.

The official version of the Boeing

According to the Pentagon, the circular hole that one observes in the third building was caused by the nose of the Boeing 757-200. Lee Evey, head of the renovation project at the Pentagon, explained it methodically during a press conference on 15 September.[1] "*The rings are E, D, C, B and A. Between B and C is*

Photo: Department of Defense

Photo: Department of Defense

a driveway that goes around the Pentagon. It's called A-E Drive. The airplane traveled in a path about like this, and the nose of the aircraft broke through this innermost wall of C ring into A-E Drive. [...] *The nose of the plane just barely broke through the inside of the C ring, so it was extending into A-E Drive a little bit. So that's the extent of penetration of the aircraft.*"

1. 'DoD News Briefing on Pentagon Renovation', op cit.

Several experts have tried to explain the official version. This version in its entirety is quite complex and deserves to be studied attentively.

– The absence of debris from the Boeing is explained by the fact that the plane was *pulverized* when it crashed into this particularly resistant building. "*The impact released extreme energy, causing the pulverization of the aircraft,*" explained an anonymous expert consulted by *Le Monde.*[1] "*The shock was such that the plane was literally pulverized,*" commented yet another anonymous specialist quoted by *Libération.*[2]

– The disappearance of the parts of the plane that are particularly resistant, such as the jet engines or the brakes, is explained by the fact that the aircraft had totally *melted* (with the exception, however, of a beacon and the black boxes found three days later[3]). "*As opposed to cars, planes are above all composed of aluminum, which starts to liquefy towards 1,050° F and the structures of the aircraft melted,*" analyzed *Le Monde.*[4] This was confirmed by *Libération*: "*Much of the plane's debris also melted in the intense heat.*"[5]

– As for the absence of one hundred tons of melted metal, this is explained by the fact that the fire attained temperatures above 4,500° F, thus causing the *evaporation* of the plane's materials (but not those of the building, nor those of the beacon and the black boxes). "*Depending on what caused it, the materials that feed it, its exposure to oxygen and its duration, a fire of this magnitude could release heat of between 3,000 and 4,500° F,"* another specialist stated. *"The heat released by the fire during 24 hours thus leads us to understand that the greater part of the plane's remains were destroyed."*[6]

– The presence of the last hole with a seven foot diameter is explained by the fact that, despite all these ordeals, the nose of the plane continued its mad course through three buildings. That is the conclusion reached by the head of the Pentagon's renovation operation.

According to the official version, the damages could thus have been produced by a Boeing 757-200. For that to have occurred, the plane was capable of *disintegrating* when it made

---

1. 'Un avion a bel et bien frappé le Pentagone' [A Plane Really Did Hit the Pentagon], *Le Monde*, 21 March 2002, op cit.
2. 'Pourquoi la démonstration de Meyssan est cousue de très gros fils blancs' blancs' [Why Meyssan's Demonstration Is a Tissue of Lies], *Libération*, 30 March 2002.
3. 'Flight Data and Cockpit Voice Recorders Found', Defense Link, Department of Defense, 14 September 2001:
4. 'Un avion a bel et bien frappé le Pentagone' [A Plane Really Did Hit the Pentagon], op cit.
5. 'Pourquoi la démonstration de Meyssan est cousue de très gros fils blancs' blancs' [Why Meyssan's Demonstration Is a Tissue of Lies], op cit.
6. Interview with Claude Moniquet, *Hoaxbuster,* 5 April 2002: http://www.hoaxbuster.com/hinterview/claude_moniquet.html

impact with the Pentagon's façade, of *melting* once it was inside the building, of *evaporating* at 4,500° F and nevertheless *perforating* two other buildings to create that hole of seven feet in diameter...[1]

The nose of a plane?

Imagine for an instant that we had not been told previously that the plane had disintegrated, melted and evaporated. Is it nevertheless possible that the nose of an airliner could have perforated three buildings and produced at its exit a perfectly circular hole seven feet wide?

The nose of a plane, the radome, contains the electronic navigation system. In order to allow passage of the waves emitted by the apparatuses, it is not made of metal, but of carbon fibers. Its form was conceived to be aerodynamic, but not particularly shock-resistant. The external envelope, as well as its contents, are thus extremely fragile. Against an obstacle, they would be crushed rather than piercing through.

---

1. We have only cited the expert testimonies most often repeated in the press. We have left aside others, like the testimony released by RTBF (the French-language public television network in Belgium) that explained the small size of the impact in this fashion: "*The wings of the plane could perfectly well have been folded back on the plane's body, which limited the point of impact.*"

One can see the fragility of plane noses in numerous pictures of crashes that were much less violent than the one that was supposed to have occurred at the Pentagon. The crash, for example, of the Boeing 757-204 of Britannia Airways in September 1999 (see page XIII of the Photo Section).

The nose is an extremely fragile shell. It is thus impossible to find the nose of the plane following such an impact. Still less could it have produced a hole as circular as that observed in the third ring of the building.

The head of a missile?

Yet, the firemen say they saw what they believed was the nose of the plane. The Boeing penetrated as far as ring C, they explain. "*The only way you could tell that an aircraft was inside was that we saw pieces of the nose gear,*" Captain Defina told the *NFPA Journal*.[1] Questioned, during a press conference at the Pentagon, about the plane's fuel, Captain Ed Plaugher answered, "*We have what we believe is a puddle right there that the — what we believe to be the nose of the aircraft...*"[2]

---

1. 'ARFF Crews Respond to the Front Line at Pentagon', *NFPA Journal*, National Fire Protection Agency, 1 November 2001: http://www.nfpa.org/NFPAJournal/onlineexclusive/Exclusive_11_01_01/exclusive_11.01.01.asp
2. 'DoD News Briefing', Defense Link, Department of Defense, 12 September 2001, op cit.

What is this piece of apparatus that was capable of inflicting such damage and that the firemen said they had observed? In contrast to the fragile nose of a plane, the heads of certain missiles are extremely resistant. This debris that firemen said they saw and that they had trouble identifying as the nose of the plane could well have been the warhead of a missile.

Now, what exactly is the damage involved here? Between the hole through which the vehicle entered and the other it created at the end of its journey, three buildings were pierced through and through. It's important to note that these three building were not *smashed into* but *pierced*. One does not in fact observe any other damage than this sort of tunnel through the Pentagon. If a Boeing 757-200 had crashed into these buildings, it would have smashed them.

The damages that it caused were in no way comparable to those of an airplane crash. The vehicle that struck the Department of Defense thus produced a very particular effect. Certain missiles are specially conceived to have a piercing effect. These missiles are weighted with depleted uranium, an extremely dense metal that heats with slightest friction and renders piercing easier. These missiles are notably used to pierce bunkers. An airplane crashes and *smashes*. A missile of this type *pierces*.

* * *

The observation of the damage that occurred thus allows us to decide between the two hypotheses of the missile or the airplane. The building was not smashed into as if it had suffered from a classic plane crash, but was perforated as if struck by a missile. To confirm the missile hypothesis, we now have to study the characteristics of the explosion and fire that followed.

THE EFFECTS OF A HOLLOW CHARGE

By Pierre-Henri Bunel[1]

What is the nature of the explosion that took place at the Pentagon on 11 September 2001? An analysis of the video pictures of the impact and the photographs of the damages permits one to know by what type of device the attack was caused. Did the explosion correspond with that produced by an airplane's kerosene or that of a real explosive? Did the fire correspond with a hydrocarbon fire or with a classic blaze?

---

1. Pierre-Henri Bunel is a graduate of the Ecole Militaire de Saint-Cyr (the French officers' academy) and a former artillery officer, whose expertise is recognized in the following fields: the effects of explosives on humans and buildings, the effects of artillery weapons on personnel and buildings, firefighting for specific types of fire, wrecks and remains of destroyed airplanes. He participated notably in the Gulf War, at the side of Generals Schwartzkopf and Roquejoffre.

Deflagration or detonation?

As a preamble, it seems indispensable to make clear to the reader an essential distinction: the difference between a deflagration and a detonation.

The combustion of explosive chemical materials – powders, explosives or hydrocarbons, for example – release energy by producing a shock wave. The diffusion at high speeds of the enormous quantity of gas produced by the chemical reaction is accompanied by flame, by a noise caused by the displacement of the shockwave through the air, and by smoke. One also often observes, even before seeing the flame, a cloud of vapor due to the compression of the air surrounding the zone of the explosion. The air can't be set into motion immediately, so it compresses under the influence of the shockwave. At first, under the compression of the air molecules, the invisible water vapor that the atmosphere always contains in greater or lesser quantities compresses and becomes visible as a white cloud.

What I would like to underline here is the notion of the shockwave. An explosion is a reaction that projects gas at a greater or lesser speeds. Explosive materials, according to their chemical composition and the physical arrangement of their molecules, impart upon the gases they generate a greater or lesser speed of propagation. One says that they are more or less progressive. The observation of the shockwave is thus a precious indication of the speed of the gases projected by the explosion.

Explosive materials are divided into two groups, according to their progressiveness. Explosives produce a shockwave whose speed of propagation is superior to a value of about six thousand feet per second. One says that they "detonate". Explosive materials whose shockwave speed is lower than that do not detonate. They deflagrate. This is the case, for example, of gunpowder or hydrocarbons.

In an internal combustion engine – and the turbojet of a Boeing 757 is a continuous internal combustion engine – the fuel under pressure deflagrates and does not detonate. If it detonated, the engine's structure would not withstand it. The kerosene of an airliner that crashes ignites and does not generally produce even deflagration, except in certain circumstances and at points limited to the engines. In the recent case of the Airbus that fell on a Queens neighborhood in New York in November 2001, the engines did not explode upon arriving at the ground. Kerosene is a heavy oil analogous to diesel fuel, tri-filtrated in order to satisfy the physical conditions of passage through the fuel injectors of jet engines. It is in no sense an explosive.

The color of explosions as also fairly remarkable. In detonations, the shockwave displaces itself rapidly. If the explosion occurs in the air without obstacles, the flame is often pale yellow at the point of the explosion. As it moves away from ground zero it turns orange then red. When it encounters obstacles, such as the walls of a building, one practically doesn't see the pale yellow part. The duration of illumination by this color is brief. The form of the flame gives an impression of "rigidity" because of the speed of propagation. It is only when the dust lifted by the shockwave starts to burn due to the brutal rise in temperature that smoke appears. This is fire smoke that has little resemblance to the black, heavy coils given off by hydrocarbon fires.

But solid explosives are not simply chemical combinations. One can improve their effectiveness by playing with their physical forms. In principle, the shockwave propagates perpendicularly to the surface undergoing reaction. By working the shapes of the explosive charges one can orient the shockwave in such a fashion as to send a maximum of energy in a given direction, like directing the light of a lighthouse with a reflector. We thus find spherical charges whose shockwaves go in all directions; cylindrical charges like those that equip shrapnel shells, those weapons that burst into minuscule pieces of steel the size of a tab of chocolate and spray the battlefield; flat charges, that allow making holes in plane obstacles with a minimum of energy lost in useless directions; but also hollow charges. These latter concentrate the principal shockwave in the shape of a high-temperature jet bearing a quantity of energy capable of piercing armor made of steel, composites or concrete.

The ignition

The explosive that constitutes the weapon[1] should explode at the desired time. In order for it to react exactly as the user wishes, it needs a certain degree of stability. The explosive that constitutes the principal charge of a weapon is too stable to explode by a simple shock. In fact, to initialize the chemical reaction, the charge must be submitted to a shockwave provoked by a more sensitive and less powerful explosive that we call the detonator. The explosive charge of the detonator reacts to a shock, to a spark or to an electrical or electromagnetic impulse. It then creates a shockwave that provokes the detonation of the principal charge.

The system that commands the explosion of the detonator is called the ignition system. The devices vary considerably and it would take too long to examine all of them. I will thus only deal with the two systems that might have been used at

1. In military language, the ammunition is the ensemble of the propulsive charge and the projectile. The weapon is the launcher for small caliber launchers, and the projectile itself for large caliber weapons systems. Thus the weapon of an artillery man is the shell or the missile, not the cannon or the launch pad.

the Pentagon, explosive ignition systems commanded by the operator and ignition systems for hollow charges by instantaneous percussion with a short delay.

Shells, bombs or missiles are equipped with an ignition system which comprises the release, the delay system and a detonator. This device is called a fuse. It is fixed on the weapon either during its construction, or at the moment of conditioning for firing. It includes a security system that prevents the ensemble from functioning until being armed.

The release can be activated by a shock in the case of percussion fuses, by a radar detector at a distance in the case of radio-electric fuses, by the reaction to a source of heat or a magnetic mass in the case of thermal or magnetic fuses.

Either the release provokes detonation instantaneously, or the delay system acts so that the weapon only detonates several milliseconds after the impact. In this last case, the weapon begins to penetrate the objective by physically denting it with its armor. The charge detonates once the weapon has already entered the objective, which increases its destructive effect.

For certain very hard fortifications, one even finds that there are multi-charge weapons. The first charges fracture the concrete, while the later one or ones penetrate and detonate. In general, anti-concrete charges are hollow charges. The jet of energy and melted materials penetrate the fortification and spread inside quantities of hot materials pushed by a column of energy that pierces the walls like a punch. The great heat produced by the detonation of the hollow charge provokes fires in everything that is combustible inside.

During the Gulf War, the anti-fortification missiles and guided bombs pierced all of the concrete bunkers that were hit, notably at Fort As Salmân. A single bomb could pierce through three thicknesses of armored concrete, having begun with the thickest, on the outside.

The missile

In order to conduct an attack with such a weapon system, a launcher is obviously needed. In the case of guided bombs, the launcher is a plane or at the very least a powerful helicopter. The weapon then leaves with an initial speed which is that of the carrier vehicle. It descends in a glide and generally guides itself by following a laser illumination. In the case of a missile, its range is much greater because the missile has its own engine. If needs be, one can conceive a system so that the missile depart from its own launch pad on the ground. There are in fact ground-to-ground anti-fortifications missiles.

A cruise missile of a recent model generally follows three phases of flight. The launch, during which it attains its flight speed in emerging from the bay of an airplane or a missile launch-tube. Pushed forward by the engine at full power, it reaches its cruising speed and deploys its wings and tail fins. It then descends to its cruising altitude and follows its approach trajectory. In the course of this flight phase, it frequently changes direction, turning according to the flight program, climbing or descending to remain low enough to escape detection as far as possible. One might then mistake it for a fighter plane in tactical flight maneuvers. It keeps this altitude until it reaches the point of entry to the terminal phase. This point is situated a certain distance from the objective; two or three miles depending on the models. From this point, the missile flies in a straight line towards the target and undergoes a strong acceleration that gives it maximum speed to strike the objective with the maximum of penetrative force.

The missile thus has to reach the point of entry to the terminal phase with great precision, so that before acceleration it is not only in the right spot but also pointing in the right direction. That is why it often happens that the missile ends its cruising flight with a tight turn that allows to adopt the right alignment. A witness might observe that the missile reduces its engine power before throttling back up.

The type of explosion observed at the Pentagon

On 8 March 2002, a month after the beginning of the controversy on Internet and three days before *The Big Lie* was published in France, five new images of the attack were released by CNN.[1] A photo agency then distributed them very widely to numerous newspapers throughout the world. These images originating from a surveillance camera were not made public by the Pentagon itself, which contented itself with authenticating them. In them, one can see the flame developing from the impact on the façade of the Department of Defense's building.

The first shot (Photo Section, p. II) is that of a white puff that seems to be a white smoke. It definitely calls to mind the vaporization of the water contained in the ambient air at the beginning of the deployment in the atmosphere of a supersonic shockwave of detonating material. One distinguishes, however, traces of red flame characteristic of the high temperatures reached by the air under the pressure of a rapid shockwave.

---

1. 'Images show September 11 Pentagon crash', *CNN*, 8 March 2002 (report includes video clip of explosion):
http://www.cnn.com/2002/US/03/07/gen.pentagon.pictures

What is plain to see is that the shock wave starts from the interior of the building. One sees above the roof the emergence of a ball of energy that isn't yet a ball of fire. One might legitimately think of a detonation by an explosive with a high energetic power, but for the moment it still cannot be determined whether it is a charge with a directed effect or not.

One distinguishes at ground level, starting from the right-hand side of the photo and going to the base of the mass of white vapor, a white line of smoke. It looks very much like the smoke that leaves the nozzle of the propulsion unit in a flying vehicle. As opposed to the smoke that would come out of two kerosene-fueled engines, this smoke is white. The turbojets of a Boeing 757 would in fact leave a trail of much blacker smoke. The examination of this photo alone already suggests a single-engine flying vehicle much smaller in size than an airliner. And without two General Electric turbo-propulsion units.

In the second shot (Photo Section, p. III) one still sees the horizontal trail of smoke but one can also make out very clearly the development of the red flame. It is interesting to compare this shot of the impact at the Pentagon with that of the impact of the plane with the second tower at the World Trade Center (Photo Section, p. III). The color of the latter is yellow, which points a lower temperature of combustion. It is mixed with black, heavy smoke. It is the color of hydrocarbon combustion in the air. In this case, it is kerosene contained in the airplane that is burning. This flame descends quite slowly down the front of the façade where the plane had penetrated, carried by the falling fuel. In contrast, the flame of the Pentagon explosion rises sharply from inside the building, ripping off debris that one sees mixed with the red flame. There is no longer the cloud of vapor due to the shockwave that masked the flame in the first photo. The intense heat has caused it to evaporate. As we have seen, that is characteristic of detonations of a high-yield explosive.

We should take the opportunity here to note the appearance of the smoke rising from the first tower that was hit, as the fire develops there. It consists of heavy, oily coils. As for traces in the air of the airplane, as opposed to the aircraft that seems to have hit the Pentagon, there is no trail although the impact has just taken place.

The photos on page IV of the color section were taken a short time after the explosion. The firemen are not yet in action. In the one at the top, the flame of the explosion itself has extinguished. The fire lit by the explosion smolders and its flames are not yet visible, except at the level of the point of impact, where one perceives a red glow in the axis of the vertical support of the highway signs. We are thus not seeing the configuration of an airliner fire because the kerosene would have ignited instantaneously. The façade has not yet collapsed. It does not present any visible signs of major mechanical destruction, although the upper floors and the roof have already been hit by the blast.

In the photo below, taken according to its author about a minute later, the fires ignited inside the building by the heat wave have begun to spread. The arrow indicates a hole in the façade through which one sees the heart of a fire beginning to mount. The façade still has not collapsed and the initial smoke has dissipated. It is only after the fires have begun to merge and form a single blaze that the thickest smoke appears, but without presenting the same appearance as the smoke from an airliner fire with its reservoirs of kerosene.

To sum up, the examination alone of these photos that everyone has seen in the press permit one to measure the striking differences between the two explosions. If the flame of the World Trade Center is obviously that of kerosene from an airplane, it would seem that this is not at all the case at the Pentagon. The flying device that struck the Department of Defense has, at first sight, nothing to do with the airliner of the official version. But we have to continue the investigation in order to progress in our search for elements that will perhaps permit us to determine the nature of the explosion that damaged the Pentagon.

A hydrocarbon fire?

When the firemen intervened on the site, one sees clearly that they are using water to attack the fire (Photo Section, p. X). Several official photographs show a fire truck that we in France would call a CCFM (*camion citerne pour feu moyen* – a tanker truck for a medium-sized fire). The water coming out of the hoses is white in color, so it does not contain that substance used on certain fires known as a "retardant". In general, retardants give the water a reddish or brownish color. Thus the principal fire being attacked is not a hydrocarbon fire, because one cannot see any foam cannons that are characteristic of interventions in airplane accidents or any hoses projecting adapted products.

However, the examination of the photo at the top of page VI does show the residues of carbonic foam. The explanation is given in certain accounts of September 11 according to which either a helicopter, for some, or a truck, for others, parked close to the façade, exploded. One can see in any case on many pictures a truck on fire to the right of the impact. On the other hand, the quantity of foam residues is relatively small. Essentially, it is spread not on the building fire but on the lawn that stretches in front, as if they had extinguished a fire set alight by that of the attack. This is what is known as a "sympathetic fire", in French firemen's jargon. A foam hose was thus used to put out one or more secondary fires.

One can see in the pictures released by the Department of Defense a truck armed with a foam cannon attacking a fire situated in front of the façade, while the high-powered water pumps attack the main fire inside the building. The spraying as it is being carried out at that moment manifestly aims at lowering the general temperature by wetting everything first, before penetrating into the building to extinguish fires point by point.

Artillery, intelligence and BDA

After having given my reactions as a former firefighter, I'm now going to give those of an artillery officer and observer. Among his tasks, an artillery observer must pick out objectives, estimate the type of weapon needed to be deployed to treat them and the quantity of projectiles required to render them harmless. Once the objective has been treated, one must still evaluate the real damage to measure whether the first strike was sufficient or if firings should continue.

It's a matter of establishing an appraisal of the damages that is then transmitted to the command and intelligence echelons. This evaluation of battlefield damages is called in English a *Battlefield Damage Assessment* (BDA). One must, of course, employ maximum objectivity in these evaluations: it would be stupid to ask for more firings on an objective that had already been neutralized or destroyed, but just as stupid to let it be thought that an objective had been rendered harmless when it still presented a menace.

During the Gulf War, every day there was a meeting in General Schwartzkopf's command post between the French, British and American commanders-in-chief. A part of the "intelligence" chapter of this briefing dealt with the examination of BDA photos. And Schwartzkopf paid particular attention to this. In these pictures one saw the effects of weapons and the scale of damage inflicted on the objectives.

This was not mere voyeurism on the part of the three generals. It permitted them to decide if there was reason to continue attacking objectives already treated, but also to decide whether to use less powerful weapons in order to prevent the destruction inflicted on military objectives from impinging on the civilian environment. Needless to say, for the interpreters of images, artillery observers and intelligence officers, damage evaluation was a key matter that we studied carefully. And when one adds practical experience to theory, as unfortunately was my case, one does possess some elements of objective appraisal in examining the damage suffered by a building; especially if one knows the building well, as is also true in my case concerning the Pentagon.

The official photos of the façade

A general view of the façade is highly interesting. Furnished again by official bodies, it is presented at the top of page V of the Photo Section.

As the firefighters finished working on the exterior of the building, one can make out several instructive elements. First of all, the soot covering the façade is a mix of that which would have been deposited in a classic fire and others more characteristic of those deposited by the shockwave of a high-yield explosive, but in no way of the thick, oily coat deposited by a kerosene fire. The windows have been broken by a detonation and not melted by a hydrocarbon fire that would have lasted several days. The most remarkable thing is that relatively few of them are broken, and that the windows affected are essentially situated close to the point of the explosion at the level of the lower floors. Near ground zero, therefore. It is very likely that the shockwave was propagated along the corridors, and one follows it very well in the general overview shown on page XI of the Photo Section. This corroborates the testimony of David Theall.[1] This liaison officer at the Pentagon describes the sudden arrival of a violent noise accompanied by debris that ravaged the corridor outside his office.

---

1. 'September 11, 2001', *Washington Post*, 16 September 2001: http://www.washingtonpost.com/ac2/wp-dyn/A38407-2001Sep15

At the beginning of its displacement, the shockwave broke panes and, once it was channeled by the walls of the corridors, it took an orientation that no longer had as much effect on the windows. It should be made clear that these were double-glazed windows in which the outer pane is particularly solid. That was what a representative of the company that installed them declared,[1] and it's also what was explained to me well before this attack, during an official visit to the Pentagon as an observer.

On a picture that is a more detailed close-up, at the bottom of page V, one has a view of the impact zone after wreckage was cleared. It allows one to make out the vertical concrete pillars of the building's frame and the corridors that run along the floors. One understands better then how the shockwave bypassed the windows as we mentioned above.

The shot shows that the vertical pillars, some of which are surrounded by wooden casings, have obviously been weakened at the ground level, that is, the place where the detonation occurred. But they weren't crushed or broken as would have been

---

1. 'DoD News Briefing on Pentagon Renovation', Defense Link, Department of Defense, 15 September 2001:
http://www.defenselink.mil/news/Sep2001/t09152001_t915evey.html

the case if they were struck by the leading edges of the wings of a hundred ton airplane. They would have been hit by the part of the leading edge situated approximately at the spot where the engine pods are fixed, the most solid area. Manifestly, no wing has struck these vertical pillars of the building's concrete frame.

If a plane had struck the Pentagon, as the official version would have us believe, the wings would have touched the vertical pillars at approximately the level of the floor on which one can see men standing. It's obvious that the weakened zone of the pillars is located below, where one can see the wooden casings and the red-colored steel props. So the vehicle that carried the charge that weakened the pillars struck lower than an enormous airliner would have done. And I refer you back to the first photographs studied on which we could see the trail of smoke from a propulsion unit very close to the ground.

This picture also permits us to put into context statements by certain experts, according to whom "the Pentagon is constructed of particularly solid materials". It's true that the building's contractors used hardened materials for the windows and the outer facings, but the Pentagon is no more a *blockhaus* than an armor-plated car is a tank.

An anti-concrete hollow charge

The last photo was produced by the Department of Defense and published on a Navy Web site.[1] It is presented on page XII of our Photo Section. In examining it, one can see an almost circular hole topped by a black smudge. This perforation is about seven feet in diameter and is situated in the wall of the third line of buildings working inward from the façade. It is supposed to have been made by the nose of the plane.

That would mean that the nose of the aircraft, a radome of carbon fiber that is far from being armored, would have traversed without destroying them six load-bearing walls of building considered to be rather solid. And what would then be the cause of the black smudge marking the wall above the hole? The hydrocarbon fire. But then, all of the façade of this building would be marked with soot and not only the few square feet that have been really blackened. And the broken windows, was that the result of the impact? I remind you that the windows are solid.

---

1. 'War and Readiness', *All Hands*, magazine of the US Navy: http://www.mediacen.navy.mil/pubs/allhands/nov01/pg16.htm

The appearance of the perforation in the wall certainly resembles the effects of anti-concrete hollow charges that I have been able to observe on a number of battlefields.

These weapons are characterized by their "jet". This jet is a mixture of gas and melted materials that is projected in the direction of the axis of the paraboloid that constitutes the forward face of the weapon. Propelled at a speed of several thousand feet per second, with a temperature of several thousands of degrees, this jet pierces concrete through many feet of thickness. It could thus pierce five thick walls of the building without any problem. Five walls out of six because the façade was perforated by the vector itself. The detonation of the military charge only occurs, in fact, once it has been carried inside the objective. As I explained earlier, the fuses arming anti-concrete charges are not instantaneous, but have a short delay. That is why the flame of the explosion developed from within the interior of the building towards the exterior. As one sees on the photos taken by the security camera, the shockwave damaged the façade, the upper floors and the roof, and propagated itself through the corridors at the height where the vector had struck: on the ground level.

The jet contains gases at a high temperature that slow and finally come to a halt before the melted materials. The gases burn everything combustible in their path. A schematic diagram of the flame and the jet of a hollow charge that is piercing walls is shown on page XIII of the Photo Section.

The melted materials travel further than the gases, and in this particular case, the picture of the last hole certainly resembles the effect that the melted materials of a jet would have had at the end of their trajectory. They would have been finally stopped by the last wall they reached. But still fairly hot enough, they would have marked the wall with this black smudge, just above the hole. Heat rises from materials that are beginning to cool and thus only mark the façade above the impact. At this terminal point, the temperature is no longer high enough to make more of a mark on the cement. On the other hand, the remnants of the shockwave still have enough energy to break the windows immediately around the hole. One understands then why the firefighters intervened with water. It is the extinguishing fluid with the strongest heat-to-mass ratio. It is thus the best-adapted to cooling materials that have absorbed a "heat wave" and to extinguish fires in urban areas that have been lit by sympathy. It was not a matter of the firefighters extinguishing a hydrocarbon fire, but of putting out punctual fires and cooling overheated materials.

This photo, and the effects described in the official version, lead me therefore to think that the detonation that struck the building was that of a high-powered hollow charge used to destroy hardened buildings and carried by an aerial vehicle, a missile.

DISAPPEARANCE OF AN AIRPLANE

On Tuesday, 11 September 2001 at 8:55 am, an airliner of the American Airlines company disappeared with sixty-four people on board. Forty-two minutes later, at 9:37 am, the defense headquarters of the United States was struck by a flying vehicle. During the day, these two events were associated: American Airlines flight 77 is said to have crashed into the Pentagon.

This version of events appears to be logical. However, when one traces back to the sources of the various items of "information" disseminated about these two events, one finds that one has no means of crosschecking them. Indeed, in tracing the threads of all the available information, one inevitably comes across one single source: the military.

A plane takes off

Information about the hijacking of the American Airlines plane linking Dulles airport in Washington to Los Angeles was not released until 10:32 am, an hour after the attack on the Pentagon, by the ABC television network.[1] No one thought at that point that this plane had crashed at the Pentagon. Ten minutes later, Fox TV claimed in fact that the Department of Defense had been struck by a US Air Force flight.

It would be another hour before the airline company confirmed the disappearance of flight 77. American Airlines announced at 11:38 am that it had lost two airliners transporting a total of 156 persons. One connected Washington to Los Angeles, and the other Boston to LA.[2] At 1:10 pm, it distributed lists of the passengers and crew members.[3]

The civilian air traffic controllers thought that a crash had occurred involving the plane that had taken off at 8:20 am. At 8:50, the pilot had his last routine communication with the control tower and, "*at 9:09 am, being unable to reach the plane by radar, the Indianapolis air controllers warned of a possible crash*", the *Washington Post* reported.[4] The terrorists, Vice-President Dick Cheney would later explain, "*turned off the transponder, which led to a later report that a plane had gone down over Ohio, but it really hadn't.*"[5]

On 12 September, it was learned that the transponder had been cut off at about 8:55 am, rendering the plane invisible to civilian air controllers who did not dispose of radars capable of picking it up in this region. The plane is said to have made a U-turn back to Washington. The source of this information is generally understood to be the civilian agency responsible for air traffic control (the Federal Aviation Authority – FAA). But the FAA could not have known that the plane turned back since it had become, by the agency's own admission, invisible to its eyes, having cut off the transponder. The "information" concerning the U-turn carried out by flight AA77 has thus no known source.

---

1. 'Minute by Minute with the Broadcast News', *Pointer.org*, 11 September 2001:
http://www.poynter.org/Terrorism/Jill1.htm
2. 'Le récit d'un jour terrible' [The Account of a Terrible Day], *Le Temps*, 12 September 2001:
http://www.letemps.ch/dossiers/dossiersarticle.asp?ID=72852
3. The lists released by Associated Press seem to be incomplete (of the 64 persons said to be aboard flight 77, only 58 names are listed). See notably on the *Washington Post* website:
http://www.washingtonpost.com/ac2/wp-dyn/A18970-2001Sep12
4. 'Pentagon Crash Highlights a Radar Gap', *Washington Post*, 3 November 2001
5. Interview of Dick Cheney in 'Meet the Press' television broadcast, *NBC*, 16 September 2001. Transcript in Appendix to *9/11 - The Big Lie*.

But why did the hijackers "*cut off the transponder*" of the aircraft, as we are told ingenuously? This operation is not only unusual during a plane hijacking: it's unheard-of. Rendering the plane's transponder inoperative is in fact the best way of raising an alert.

The procedures are very strict in the case of a problem with a transponder, both on the civilian side and the military. The FAA's regulations describe exactly how to proceed when a transponder is not functioning properly: the control tower should enter into radio contact at once with the pilot and, if it fails, immediately warn the military who would then send fighters to establish visual contact with the crew.[1] But the interruption of a transponder also directly sets off an alert with the military body responsible for the air defenses of the United States and Canada, the North American Aerospace Defense Command (NORAD). The transponder is the plane's identity card. An aircraft that does not dispose of this identification is immediately monitored. "*If an object has not been identified in less than two minutes or appears suspect, it is considered to be an eventual threat,*" officials explain. "*Unidentified planes, planes in distress and planes we suspect are being used for illegal activities can then be intercepted by a fighter from NORAD.*"[2] The interception of airplanes was part of the "*routine*", added a spokesman of this organization.[3]

According to the official version, the pirates thus gave the alert themselves by cutting off the Boeing's transponder forty minutes before they struck the Pentagon. No one has been capable of explaining the reasons for this curious tactic.

The interruption of a transponder can eventually produce another effect beyond setting off alarms: it renders the plane invisible to civilian air controllers. In certain regions, these controllers do have radars, called "primaries", that are able to detect air movements. The radars they normally use are called "secondaries" and limit themselves to recording the signals emitted by the transponders of airplanes (registration, altitude, etc.). Cutting off the transponder thus permits one to vanish from these "secondary" radars, and only appear on the primary ones. According to the FAA, the air controllers did not have access to primary radars in Ohio.[4] That's why the plane totally disappeared from their screens.

---

1. See FAA regulations: http://faa.gov/ATpubs
And notably those concerning the hijacking of a plane and military operations: http://faa.gov/ATpubs/MIL
2. 'NORAD: Une journée de mission' [NORAD: A Day's Mission], Web site of the National Defence of Canada:
http://www.airforce.dnd.ca/athomedocs/athome1e_f.htm
3. 'Facing Terror Attack's Aftermath: Otis Fighter Jets Scrambled Too Late to Halt the Attacks', *Boston Globe*, 15 September 2001, page A1:
http://www.boston.com/news/packages/underattack/pdf/091501.pdf
4. See notably 'Pentagon Crash Highlights a Radar Gap', op cit.

Why then deactivate the aircraft's transponder? To set off an alert or to make the plane invisible to civilians alone?

From the moment flight AA77 disappeared, officially at around 8:55 am, all information about it comes exclusively from military sources. The FBI even ordered the civil aviation authorities not to divulge any information concerning this plane. "*Details about who was on flight 77, when it took off and what happened on board were tightly held by airline, airport and security officials last night,*" the *Washington Post* explained. "*All said that the FBI had asked them not to divulge details.*"[1]

From civilian sources we thus know very few things: an American Airlines plane took off from Dulles airport in Washington at 8:20 am bound for Los Angeles on the other side of the country. The last radio contact with the pilot took place at 8:50. The air traffic controllers lost all contact with the aircraft before 9:09, the time when they raised the alert of a possible crash.

1. 'On Flight 77: Our Plane Is Being Hijacked', *Washington Post*, 12 September 2001:
http://www.washingtonpost.com/ac2/wp-dyn/A14365-2001Sep11

From military sources, we learn all the rest: the air traffic controllers had lost radar contact with the plane, because its transponder was turned off at 8:55. Out of their sight, the plane turned around and finally plunged into the Pentagon, a few miles from its point of departure, one hour and seventeen minutes later, after having traveled nearly 600 miles.

Yet, nothing indicated at the start that an eventual link existed between the vehicle that struck the Pentagon and flight AA77.

The attack on the Pentagon: plane, helicopter or bomb?

Nearly three-quarters of an hour after the crashes of two planes into the World Trade Center in New York, the federal capital, Washington, was also hit. A first attack seems to have taken place in an annex of the White House, the Old Executive Office Building. At 9:42 am, the ABC television network showed pictures of thick smoke coming out of this US presidential building. These furtive pictures were soon forgotten, eclipsed two minutes later by the announcement of a second fire, this time at the American defense headquarters, the Pentagon. The information released at the time by the television networks and press agencies was contradictory. For some, the fire was caused by a booby-trapped vehicle, others believed it was another plane hijacking, and a third group announced a helicopter crash.

Shortly before 10 am, the first press release from the Department of Defense mentions an "*attack*" but does not give details as to its nature.[1]

At the White House, the situation was not any clearer. In the first hours, the National Security adviser, Condoleezza Rice, only knew that "*something*" had struck the Pentagon. "*It was pretty remarkable in those first few hours, coming out of the Situation Room. We had just heard that there was a second plane* [that flew] *into the World Trade Tower. And coming out, we heard something had hit the Pentagon and that something was likely headed for the White House.*"[2] Vice President Cheney was not better informed. He explained that "*the first reports on the Pentagon attack suggested a helicopter and then later a private jet.*"[3]

---

1. This press release was removed from the DoD website, but can be consulted on that of the University of Yale:
http://www.yale.edu/lawweb/avalon/sept_11/dod_brief03.htm
2. 'Rice gained first-hand experience when front line of terror closed in', *Chicago Tribune*, 14 September 2001:
http://www.chicagotribune.com/templates/misc/printstory.jsp?slug=chi%2D0109140367sep14
3. 'Jets Had Bush OK to Down Airliners', *Los Angeles Times*, 17 September 2001:
http://www.latimes.com/templates/misc/printstory.jsp?slug=la%2D091701shoot

The first to speak of an airplane was the Secretary of Defense, Donald Rumsfeld. Just after the attack, he left his office to observe the damage. "*When he came back in the building about half an hour later,*" his assistant, Victoria Clarke said, "*he was the first one that told us he was quite sure it was a plane. Based on the wreckage and based on the thousands and thousands of pieces of metal. He was the one that told us, the staff that was in the room. So he was really the first one who told us that it was most likely a plane.*"[1]

Strange. The highest political leaders of the land are placed under shelter in protected chambers, like Condoleezza Rice and Dick Cheney, who were taken to the underground bunker of the White House. The American defense headquarters is attacked without anyone being able to say how it happened. The situation is confusing, and dangerous. Yet the Secretary of Defense goes outside immediately after the attack to inspect the damage and explain that it's an airplane that crashed into the Pentagon.

---

1. Interview with Victoria Clarke, *WBZ Boston Saturday*, 15 September 2001:
http://www.defenselink.mil/news/Sep2001/t09162001_t0915wbz.html

The information service of the armed forces rapidly lets it be known, on the Pentagon's Web site, that was a "*commercial airliner, possibly hijacked.*"[1] But during the first official press conference at the Department of Defense, the spokesman for the Navy, Rear Admiral Craig Quigley, said he did not have information concerning what was termed the "*allegedly hijacked commercial aircraft*"[2]

In the afternoon, the connection with American Airlines flight 77 was suggested to the press by anonymous military personnel. This "information" then spread among the media like a rumor. Only the *Los Angeles Times* specified its sources: it reported that officials "*speaking under the condition of anonymity*" explained to journalists that the Pentagon had been hit by flight 77.[3]

However, no civilian source came to confirm these off-the-record remarks by the military. The air traffic controllers at Dulles airport in Washington disposed of primary radars but could only state that they had picked up an unidentified aircraft flying at high speed towards the capital. "*The first Dulles controller noticed the fast-moving plane at 9:25 a.m. Moments later, controllers sounded an alert that an aircraft appeared to be headed directly toward the White House.*"[4] One of them, Danielle O'Brien, then explained that, "*The speed, the maneuverability, the way that he turned, we all thought in the radar room, all of us experienced air*

Photo : Boeing / www.boeing.com

Boeing 757-200 or missile?

"I saw a American Airlines jet coming very quickly and at low altitude."
Infantry Captain Lincoln Liebner, *AFP*, 12 September 2001

"The airplane seemed to be able to hold between eight or twelve persons."
Steve Patterson, *Washington Post*, 11 September 2001, 4:59 pm

"We heard something that made the sound of a missile, then we heard a powerful boom."
Tom Seibert, *Washington Post*, 11 September 2001, 4:59 pm

"A plane, a plane from American Airlines. I thought: 'That's not right, it's really low'. And I saw it. I mean, it was like a cruise missile with wings."
Mike Walter, *CNN*, 12 September 2001

"A silver airplane with the distinctive marks along the windows that made me say that was an American Airlines plane."
Joel Sucherman, *eWeek*, 13 September 2001

"The speed, the maneuverability, the way that he turned, we all thought in the radar room, all of us experienced air traffic controllers, that that was a military plane."
Danielle O'Brien, *ABCNews*, 24 October 2001

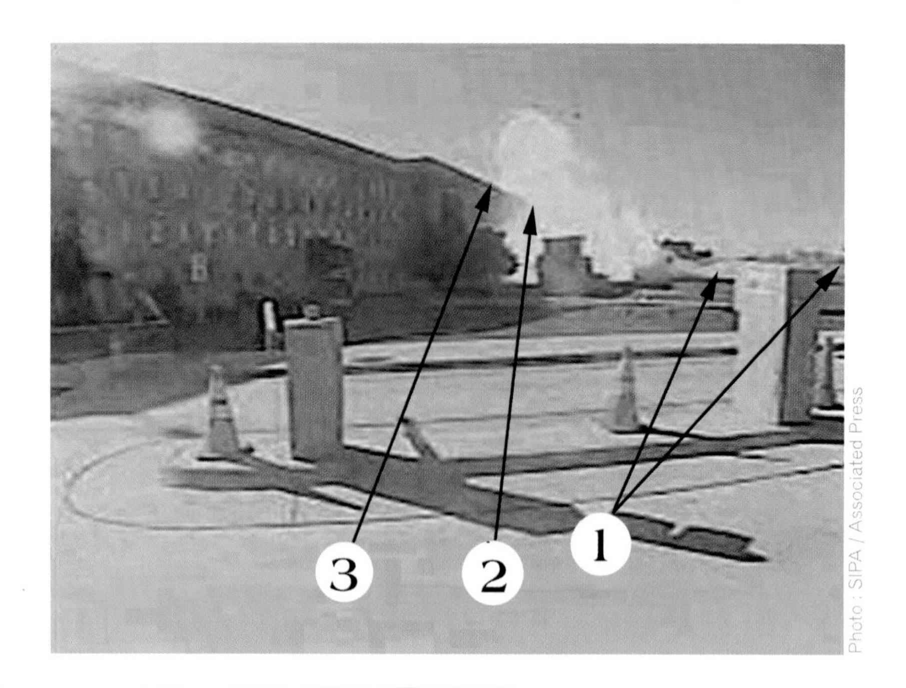

Detonation or deflagration?
Explosive materials are divided into two groups, according to their progressiveness. Explosives produce a shockwave whose speed of propagation is superior to a value of about six thousand feet per second. One says that they "detonate". Explosive materials whose shockwave speed is lower than that do not detonate. They deflagrate. This is the case, for example, of gunpowder or hydrocarbons.

This image of the impact on the Pentagon is very instructive as to the nature of the explosion. Under the pressure of the shockwave, the water contained in the ambient air is compressed and forms a cloud of vapor. The speed of propagation on the shockwave is very high. It corresponds to a detonation of an explosive with high energetic power. The explosion does not correspond to a deflagration of kerosene.

1. Trail of smoke from a propulsion unit.
2. Cloud of water vapor under pressure.
3. The explosion develops from inside the building.

Photo : SIPA / Associated Press

Pentagon
Development of the flame. The color is not that of a hydrocarbon flame in open air.

Photo : Associated Press

World Trade Center
The yellow color is the sign of a lower temperature of combustion.
The flame is mixed with black, heavy smoke. It is that of the combustion of the hydrocarbons in the air.

The flame descends, fairly slowly, in front of the façade.
That of the Pentagon, in contrast, rises suddenly from inside the building.

The fire smolders

This picture was taken very shortly after the explosion. The firemen are not yet in action. The flame of the explosion is extinguished. The fire lit by the explosive smolders and the flames are not yet visible, except at the level of the point of impact (at the place of the red glow, in the axis of the vertical support of the highway sign). We are not in the configuration of an airliner fire because the kerosene would have gone up in flames instantaneously.

The start of a classic urban fire

About a minute later, the fires alight inside the building by the heat wave begin to grow in scale. The arrow indicates a hole in the façade through which one sees the heart of a fire beginning to mount. The initial smoke has dissipated. Shortly after, the fires have begun to merge and form a single blaze.

Photo : Department of Defense

The soot and the windows

The soot covering the façade is a mixture that corresponds to a classic fire and to a shockwave of a high-yield explosive. It is in no way the thick, oily coat deposited by a kerosene fire.
The windows have been broken by a detonation and not melted by a hydrocarbon fire that would have lasted several days. Few of them are broken.
The windows affected are essentially situated close to the point of the explosion at the level of the lower floors.

Photo : Department of Defense

The building frame

The vertical pillars, certain of which are surrounded by wooden casings, have been weakened. But they haven't been crushed or broken by the leading edge of the wings of an airplane weighing one hundred tons. They would indeed been hit by the part of the leading edge situated at about the point where the engines are fixed, that is, the most solid area.
If an airliner had hit the Pentagon, the wings would touched the vertical pillars at about the level where the men are standing. The weakened area of the pillars is situated below.

Intervention of the first emergency crews at the impact site

These photos were taken between 9:40 and 10:10 am. The façade has not yet collapsed. One distinguishes the hole by which the aircraft entered, between the ground and first floors (see enlargement on the right-hand page).

A secondary fire has started on the right: a truck parked in front of the Pentagon has caught fire. The smoke that escapes is that of a hydrocarbon fire.

Photo : U.S. Marine Corps, Cpl. Jason Ingersoll

Enlargement of the impact
The orifice by which the "Boeing" entered measures about 15 to 18 feet wide. The wall above is intact. It was not hit by the tail of a Boeing 757-200. The lawn is intact, the aircraft not having touched the ground. According to the Department of Defense, the "plane" arrived at an angle of about 45°.
A Boeing 757-200 has a cabin 10.5 feet wide in diameter and a wingspan of 114 feet. The jet engines are fixed to the wings and constitute two of the most solid elements of the aircraft. When the landing gear is not extended, the Boeing measures a little over 36 feet in height with the tail.

Photo : U.S. Army, Sgt. Carmen L. Burgess

The aircraft was swallowed by the building

The photograph above shows the façade as it collapses, toward 10:10 am. According to many witnesses, the aircraft disappeared into the interior of the building. One observes in fact that the device did not touch the lawn.

Photo : U.S. Army, Sgt. Carmen L. Burgess

Photo : U.S. Army, Sgt. Carmen L. Burgess

A hydrocarbon fire?

One observes two types of smoke. In front of the building, a thick black smoke is comming from a truck that caught fire. From the building itself rises gray smoke. The first does correspond to a hydrocarbon fire. But the other, the main fire, corresponds to a classic urban fire. In the picture to the right, the truck fire has been put out.

Photo : Jim Garamone, American Forces Press Service

Photo : Jim Garamone, American Forces Press Service

The explosion took place in the interior

The fire propagated rapidly in the interior of the building, along the corridors, as one observes in the overview photo below. Outside, a secondary fire started with the explosion of a trucked that was parked slightly to the right of the impact. The explosion however did not touch the heliport turret, barely further away on the left. It was thus inside and not outside that the explosion had its greatest effect.

Photo : DoD, Tech. Sgt. Cedric H. Rudisill

Photo : Department of Defense / www.mediacen.navy.mil

A hole seven feet wide

According to the Department of Defense, this photograph represents *"the exit orifice marking the place where American Airlines flight 77 ended its penetration of the Pentagon."* This hole of about seven feet is said to have been made by *"the nose of the plane"*.

Photo : Josep Duran / Airliners.net

The nose of a Boeing
A nose of a Boeing of the same type as that said to have caused the hole, but after a much less serious crash than that supposed to have occurred at the Pentagon. The nose - or radome - is a very fragile shell containing electronic navigation devices.
The cabin of the plane measures about 10.5 feet in diameter.

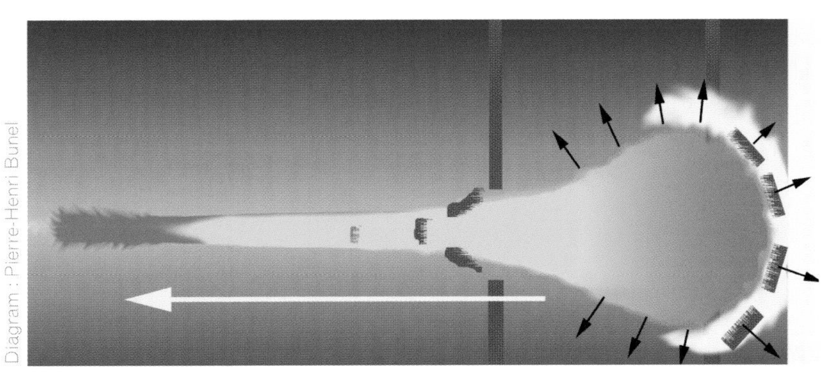

Diagram : Pierre-Henri Bunel

Diagram of the action of a hollow charge
By working the shapes of explosive charges, one can orientate the shockwave in a fashion to send the maximum energy in a given direction. Hollow charges concentrate the principal shockwave in the form a high temperature jet that carries a quantity of energy capable of piercing armour made of steel, composites, or concrete.
The white arrow indicates the direction of the jet's projection. The black arrows represent the secondary shockwave. All of the shockwaves rip away debris that becomes burning projectiles.

Three pierced buildings
These photographs show the emplacement of the hole (see cover photo) caused by the aircraft.
The device penetrated into the Pentagon at an angle of about 45° until the façade of the third building.
The three buildings have been pierced from one side to the other.
The haven't been smashed into as would be the case if had been a plane crash.

According to the official version, a Boeing weighing over 100 tons with a wingspread of 114 feet traversed the three buildings.

The orifice by which it entered, rectangular in shape, measures 15 to 18 feet wide. The exit hole, circular in form measures 7 feet in diameter.

The Boeing is said to have been "gasified" at 5,400° F, at the ground level of the building, without having damaged the upper floors.

The white arrow represents the trajectory of the aircraft, and its point, the place where "it's nose came out".

Source photo : www.geoffmetcalf.com

Photo : Mark Faram / SIPA - Associated Press

"Evidence" of the plane

Numerous newspapers have reproduced this shot assuring that it represents a piece of debris from American Airlines flight 77.

Yet, this piece of sheet metal does not correspond with any piece of a Boeing 757-200 painted in the colors of American Airlines. It has not moreover been inventoried by the Department of Defense as coming from flight 77.

traffic controllers, that that was a military plane." [5]

These civilian sources thus confirmed than an unidentified aircraft, flying at high speed and with great maneuverability was headed for Washington. But on the other hand, they didn't say that it was a Boeing 757-200 and still less that it belonged to the American Airlines company. On the contrary, they thought it was a military aircraft.

It was therefore neither the civilian air traffic controllers nor the airline company that identified this vehicle as being flight AA77. The identification of the aircraft was made entirely by the army. Once again, the sole source is military.

---

1. 'Alleged Terrorist Airliner Attack Targets Pentagon', *American Forces Information Service*, Defense Link, DoD, 11 September 2001: http://www.defenselink.mil/news/Sep2001/n09112001_200109111.html
2. 'DoD Official Provides Briefing After Pentagon Attack', *American Forces Information Service*, Defense Link, DoD, 11 September 2001:
http://www.defenselink.mil/news/Sep2001/n09112001_200109113.html
3. 'Hijacked Jets Fly into Trade Center, Pentagon', *Los Angeles Times*, 11 September 2001:
http://www.latimes.com/templates/misc/printstory.jsp?slug=la%2D091101leadall
4. 'Pentagon Crash Highlights a Radar Gap', *Washington Post*, op cit.
5. 'Get These Planes on the Ground', *ABCNews*, 24 October 2001: www.abcnews.go.com/sections/2020/2020/2020_011024_atc_feature.html

Official testimony

On 12 September, however, a civilian source did seem to come forward to confirm the vision of military officials. It was learned that Barbara Olsen, former federal prosecutor and star commentator on CNN during Bill Clinton's impeachment proceedings, was in the plane and contacted her husband, Theodore, twice in the moments before the attack on the Pentagon. The testimony is succinct, but it confirms that the plane was hijacked and had not crashed in Ohio as the air traffic controllers initially believed.

This testimony nevertheless requires caution. In the first place, it's third-hand testimony: it was not initially reported by the person who received it, but by a friend of the family and CNN journalist, Tim O'Brien. The latter reported what Theodore Olson said his wife had told him. Secondly, Theodore Olson, Solicitor General of the United States, is very close to the Bush administration, of which he constitutes an essential support each time a major legal difficulty arises. For example, it was he who pleaded George W. Bush's cause when the Supreme Court had to rule on the Presidential elections of 2000. It was again he who defended Vice President Cheney over refusing to transmit documents to Congress in the investigation of the Enron scandal. And Mr. Olson himself declared before the Supreme

Court of the United States that, "*It is easy to imagine an infinite number of situations ... where government officials might quite legitimately have reasons to give false information out.*"[1]

Many people have interpreted this testimony as being a confirmation of the crash of flight AA77 at the Pentagon. However, nothing in Barbara Olson's words permit such conclusions to be drawn. The testimony is cited a first time in an article by Tim O'Brien published on CNN's Internet site, on 12 September at 2:06 am. One only learns from this that the plane was hijacked and the pirates were armed with cutters: "*Barbara Olson, a conservative commentator and attorney, alerted her husband, Solicitor General Ted Olson, that the plane she was on was being hijacked Tuesday morning, Ted Olson told CNN.* [...] *Her husband said she called him twice on a cell phone from American Airlines Flight 77, which was en route from Washington Dulles International Airport to Los Angeles. [...] Ted Olson told CNN that his wife said all passengers and flight personnel, including the pilots, were herded to the*

1. 'This president thinks our ignorance is bliss', *Yahoo! News*, 22 March 2001:
http://story.news.yahoo.com/news?tmpl=story&u=/020323/79/1ao0k.html

back of the plane by armed hijackers. The only weapons she mentioned were knives and cardboard cutters. [...] *She felt nobody was in charge and asked her husband to tell the pilot what to do.*"[1]

Barbara Olson's testimony was reported a second time in the *Washington Post* of 12 September 2001. One didn't learn anything new, except that she hadn't given any details as to the identity or number of hijackers: "*Her last words to him were,* 'What do I tell the pilot to do?' [...] 'She called from the plane while it was being hijacked,' *Theodore Olson said.* 'I wish it wasn't so, but it is.' [...] *The two conversations each lasted about a minute, said Tim O'Brien, a CNN reporter and friend of the Olsons. In the first call, Barbara Olson told her husband,* 'Our plane is being hijacked.' *She described how hijackers forced passengers and the flight's pilot to the rear of the aircraft. She said nothing about the number of hijackers or their nationality.* [...] *Olson's first call was cut off, and her husband immediately called the Justice Department's command center, where he was told officials knew nothing about the Flight 77 hijacking.* [...] *Moments later, his wife called again. And again, she wanted to know,* 'What should I tell the pilot?' 'She was composed, as composed as you can be under the circumstances,' *O'Brien said.* [...] *But her second call was cut off, too.*"[2]

Six months later, on 5 March 2002, Theodore Olson himself quoted his wife's words in a British newspaper, the *Family Telegraph*. He was watching the attacks on the World Trade Center when his wife phoned. " *'Someone rushed in and told me what had happened. I went into the other room, where there's a television,' Olson says. 'It went through my mind,* "My God, maybe – Barbara's on an airplane, and two airplanes have been crashed," *you know.' Then his secretary told him that Barbara was on the line. 'My first reaction when I heard she was on the phone was relief, because I knew that she wasn't on one of those two airplanes.' But Barbara then explained calmly that she had been herded to the back of the Boeing 757 she was on, along with the other passengers. 'She had had trouble getting through, because she wasn't using her cellphone, she was using the phone in the passengers' seats,' says Olson. 'I guess she didn't have her purse, because she was calling collect, and she was trying to get through to the Department of Justice, which is never very easy.' He was able to tell her about the World Trade Center attacks before the line went*

---

1. 'Wife of Solicitor General alerted him of hijacking from plane', by Tim O'Brien, *CNN*, 12 September 2001:
http://www.cnn.com/2001/US/09/11/pentagon.olson
2. 'On Flight 77: "Our Plane Is Being Hijacked"', *Washington Post*, 12 September 2001:
http://www.washingtonpost.com/ac2/wp-dyn/A14365-2001Sep11

dead, then he called his departmental command center to let them know another plane had been hijacked. The phone rang again and it was Barbara. 'She wanted to know, "What can I tell the pilot? What can I do? How can I stop this?" *I tried to find out where she thought she was – I wanted to know where the airplane was and what direction it was going in, because I thought that was the first step to being able to do something. We both tried to reassure one another that everything was going to be OK, she was still alive, the plane was still up in the air. But I think she knew that it wasn't going to be OK and I knew it wasn't going to be OK.' They were able to have "personal exchanges", he says, before they were cut off in mid-conversation. 'It just stopped. It could be the impact, although I think she would have... There's no point in speculating.' As soon as he heard a plane had crashed at the Pentagon, he says, 'I knew it was her'."*[1]

This new version is more precise, but one still doesn't know where the plane was. Theodore Olson explained that he wanted to know "*where the airplane was and what direction it was going in*". It

---

1. 'She asked me how to stop the plane', *Family Telegraph*, 5 March 2002:
http://www.telegraph.co.uk/family/main.jhtml?xml=%2Ffamily%2F2002%2F03%2F05%2Ffolsen05.xml

is possible to suppose that the plane in which Barbara found herself crashed into the Pentagon. It nevertheless remains a supposition. Her husband is convinced of it, but nothing in the testimony that he received points to that. Barbara Olson only indicated one thing: at 8:55 am, the plane had not crashed but had been hijacked. This source thus does not confirm that flight AA77 was headed for the federal capital, as the army claims.

* * *

The Secretary of Defense, Donald Rumsfeld, was the first to declare that a plane had crashed into the Pentagon. Later, military officials told us with greater details the presumed history of flight AA77. But the army is the sole source that we have. The civilian sources tell us something else: according to the control tower in Indianapolis, the plane and its sixty-four passengers and crew members vanished shortly before 9 am. It seems, according an indirect testimony, that the Boeing hadn't crashed, but had been hijacked. Other than that, at 9:25 am an unidentified aircraft whose speed and maneuverability made the air traffic controllers think of a "*military plane*" was headed for Washington and struck the Department of Defense.

Can one affirm that it was in fact American Airlines flight 77 that hit the Pentagon? Only if one has blind faith in the army of the United States of America.

THE OFFICIAL PARADOX

The official version raises a certain number of questions that have not escaped many political leaders. The latter are aware that nearly three-quarters of an hour elapsed between the interruption of the transponder and the crash of the plane. Why, then, wasn't the plane intercepted by military fighters? Why didn't the Air Force protect Washington?

The military on the defensive

Having just been appointed Chairman of the Joint Chiefs-of-Staff by President Bush, General Myers was auditioned, on 13 September, by the Senate. The Armed Services Committee was meeting to confirm his appointment. This hearing had been scheduled for some time and did not focus on the reaction of the army to the attacks of 11 September. However, the general was also questioned about this matter. Myers tried then to clear the military of responsibility for the events. In order to explain why flight 77 was not shot down, he let it be understood that the orders to the fighters to take off were given "*to the best of my knowledge, after the Pentagon was struck.*"[1] Without fear of contradiction, he also asserted that, "*When it became clear what the threat was, we did scramble fighter aircraft, AWACS, radar aircraft and tanker aircraft to begin to establish orbits in case other aircraft showed up in the FAA system that were hijacked.* [...] *At the time of the first impact on the World Trade Center, we stood up our crisis action team. That was done immediately.*"

But General Myer's statement did not close the debate entirely. According to his remarks, the military did in fact wait nearly three-quarters of an hour before ordering fighters to take off.

Two days later, on 15 September, NORAD issued a contradictory press release. It published the chronology of the times at which it said it had been notified of the hijackings by the FAA and had given the takeoff orders to the fighters: NORAD said it hadn't been informed of the hijacking of flight 77 until 9:24 am and then had immediately given

1. Senate audition of General Myers, 13 September 2001. Excerpts published in *9/11 - The Big Lie*.

orders to two F-16's to take off. These were effectively in flight by 9:30. Too late to prevent the crash that occurred at 9:37 (the previous estimations by the Pentagon spoke of 9:38, those of the *Washington Post*, CNN, ABC and CBS timed it at 9:41 am).

This version of events lets all of the responsibility for the disaster be borne by the FAA, for having waited twenty-nine minutes before warning the military authorities. But it also seems implausible concerning the military's reactions.

When the transponder cut off, why didn't the military locate the plane themselves and engage the interception procedure as is common practice for them? Doesn't the army have its own radars? Because if certain civilian radars couldn't "see" the planes whose transponders were cut off, this is not the case of military radars, which pick up all types of aircraft.

Why were fighters sent from Langley base in Virginia, and not from Saint Andrews? The first is 105 miles from the Pentagon, whereas as the second is only 10 miles.

Why were two F-16's sent rather than F-15's? The first fly at 1,500 mph, whereas the second are faster, at 1,875 mph. Why were the slower planes chosen?

Why were fighters sent instead of a missile? Shouldn't the military have attempted to destroy the plane? If they had wanted to destroy a hostile aircraft, they had missiles available that were much faster.

Moreover, independently of the interception of flight 77, the crisis situation called for maximum air defense protection over the capital and thus the positioning of fighters in flight over Washington. This elementary precaution fell to the Presidential airbase at Saint Andrews. It could have prevented the attack on the Pentagon, but it was not carried out. Yet, a half-hour before the attack on the Pentagon, General Eberhart, commander-in-chief of NORAD, had activated the SCATANA plan and taken control of the New York airspace in order to position fighters there.

For the military, from the moment when they were alerted of flight AA77's disappearance, it was no longer a question of knowing whether they were facing a simple technical incident. The factual elements that they disposed of were sufficiently precise: several tens of minutes after terrorist attacks using airliners as missiles, the transponder of a plane is cut off, the pilot fails to respond, the aircraft deviates from its flight course, and lastly, heads at high speed towards the country's capital. The job of the military could not be clearer: shoot down the hostile aircraft as soon as possible. The version presented by NORAD had perhaps as its objective to let the FAA take the responsibility. But doesn't it also show without ambiguity that the army had no intention of shooting down a plane headed for Washington, despite whatever menace it seemed to represent?

The president comes to the rescue of the military

The day after the publication of this chronology, Vice President Dick Cheney tried to justify the military's incapacity by the fact that shooting down a civilian airplane would be "*a decision left up to the President*".[1] By insisting on the gravity of the decision, as it implicated the death of "*American citizens*", Dick Cheney let it be understood that the president would not have taken it hastily. And the Vice President insisted on the risks that weighed on George W. Bush himself, whose plane was also a target according to the Secret Service. Everyone could imagine that on a day of such panic and confusion, it was not impossible that a decision had been a little late in coming.

However, the Vice President's claim is false. In the first place, he assimilates the interception of an airplane with the decision to shoot it down. Intercepting an aircraft means that the fighters establish *visual contact* with the plane and give it orders with luminous

1. Interview with Dick Cheney on 'Meet the Press', *NBC*, 16 September 2001.

signals. Shooting down a plane means that fighters *already positioned* receive the order to open fire. Secondly, Dick Cheney claims erroneously that this order could only be given by the President himself.

The interception of a suspect civilian aircraft by fighters is automatic and does not require any kind of political decision-making. It should have taken place on 11 September, when the transponder was cut off. Whether or not they received the order to shoot down the plane, the fighters should have taken off immediately.

The order to open fire comes at a second moment. But one greatly wonders what regulations Dick Cheney is referring to in order to claim that this decision belongs to the President. Because the regulations concerning airplane hijackings and the destruction of flying vehicles in fact confide that responsibility to the Secretary of Defense: " [*With the exception of urgent requests needing an immediate response and foreseen within regulations the NMCC* [National Military Command Center] *transmits all requests for military assistance to the Secretary of Defense for accord.*]"[1]

The official responsible in these matters is thus the Secretary of Defense "*with exceptions*". These exceptions are none other the necessity of saving human lives faced with imminent danger. "[*It is possible to formulate to any element in the chain of command 'Requests needing Immediate*

Response'. These arise from imminently serious conditions where only an immediate action taken by an official of the Department of Defense or a military commander can prevent loss of lives, or mitigate human suffering and great property damage.]" [2]

In other terms, the decision to shoot down flight AA77 was not up to President Bush. It did not depend either on Secretary of Defense Rumsfeld. This decision belonged first of all to the military officials, in the front ranks of whom was General Ralph Eberhardt, commander-in-chief of NORAD.

---

1. The regulations were modified three months before the attack. First version: 'Aircraft Piracy (Hijacking) and Destruction of Derelict Airborne Objects', Chairman of the Joint Chiefs of Staff, 31 July 1997 (CJCSI 3610.01):
http://www.dtic.mil/doctrine/jel/cjcsi/361001a.pdf
Second version: 'Aircraft Piracy (Hijacking) and Destruction of Derelict Airborne Objects', Chairman of the Joint Chiefs of Staff, 1 June 2001 (CJCSI3610.01A):
http://www.dtic.mil/doctrine/jel/cjcsd/cjcsi/361001a.pdf
2. 'Military Support to Civil Authorities (MSCA)', DoD Directive 3025.1, 15 January 1993:
http://www.dtic.mil/whs/directives/corres/html/30251.htm
'Military Assistance to Civil Authorities', DoD Directive 3025.15, 18 February 1997:
http://www.nci.org/publications/32%20dod%20305.15.pdf

The further one progresses in the investigation, the more the military have difficulties in justifying the official version. The new military chief of staff pretends not to know this. NORAD tries to buy time but doesn't manage to explain the absence of a military response. And lastly, the Vice President tries to make people believe that it involved too high a level for the order to be given immediately. Each new statement poses new questions. We will see that the more the phantom plane approaches the Pentagon, the more the explanations of the military become incoherent.

The Pentagon fails to react

Five extremely sophisticated antimissile batteries protect the headquarters of the army of the United States from any airborne attack. How can one explain the fact that this anti-aircraft defense was not used?

According to a Pentagon spokesman, Lieutenant-Colonel Vic Warzinski, the military had not been expecting such an attack. "*The Pentagon was simply not aware that this aircraft was coming our way*", he claimed.[1]

This explanation is simply not credible: the Pentagon knew full well that an unidentified flying vehicle was speeding toward Washington. On 11 September, in fact; communications between civilian air traffic controllers and the various federal authorities functioned perfectly. Besides, the controllers were not only in direct contact with the Pentagon, but also with the White House. From 9:25 am, the control tower at Dulles airport observed a vehicle flying towards the capital. "*Dulles controllers spotted an unidentified aircraft speeding directly toward the restricted airspace that surrounds the White House.*", reported the Washington Post.[2] One of these controllers, Danielle O'Brien, who we already quoted above, confirmed this episode and added, "*it was just a countdown. Ten miles west. Nine miles west ... Our supervisor picked up our line to the White House and started relaying to them the information,* [that] *we have an unidentified very fast-moving aircraft inbound toward your vicinity, 8 miles west.* [...] *And it went six, five, four. And I had it in my mouth to say, three, and all of a sudden the plane turned away. In the room, it was almost a sense of relief. This must be a fighter. This*

1. 'Air Attack on Pentagon Indicates Weaknesses', *Newsday*, 23 September 2001:
http://www.newsday.com/ny-uspent232380681sep23.story
2. 'On Flight 77: "Our Plane Is Being Hijacked"', *Washington Post*, 12 September 2001:
http://www.washingtonpost.com/ac2/wp-dyn/A14365-2001Sep11

must be one of our guys sent in, scrambled to patrol our capital, and to protect our president, and we sat back in our chairs and breathed for just a second [...] *We lost radar contact with that aircraft. And we waited. And we waited. And your heart is just beating out of your chest waiting to hear what's happened* [...] *And then the Washington National* [Airport] *controllers came over our speakers in our room and said,* 'Dulles, hold all of our inbound traffic. The Pentagon's been hit.' "[1]

Vice President Cheney confirmed, moreover, that "*the Secret Service has an arrangement with the FAA, they had open lines,*" once the World Trade Center was hit.[2] For another thing, the FAA officials were constantly present within the Saint Andrews military base, which is entrusted with the protection of the capital. "*Federal Aviation Administration personnel at Andrews are responsible for the airway facilities and air traffic control over and around Andrews,*" explains the base's Internet site. "*The FAA men and women control and service the vast and complex network of air navigation and air traffic control facilities as part of the national airspace system. Their mission is the safe movement of air traffic in the nation's airspace.*"[3] The military in Washington were thus immediately given the information available to the FAA, twelve minutes before the attack.

But the army did not have to wait for the FAA's warning to know that a vehicle was heading for the capital. It possesses in fact several very sophisticated radar monitoring systems, incomparable with the civilian systems. The PAVE PAWS system is, for example, used essentially detect and track objects difficult to pick up such as missiles flying at very low altitudes. PAVE PAWS does not miss anything occurring in North American airspace: "*The radar system is capable of detecting and monitoring a great number of targets that would be consistent with a massive SLBM* [Submarine Launched Ballistic Missile] *attack. The system must rapidly discriminate between vehicle types, calculating their launch and impact points in addition to the scheduling, data processing and communications requirements.*"[4]

---

1. 'Get These Planes on the Ground', *ABCNews*, 24 October 2001: www.abcnews.go.com/sections/2020/2020/2020_011024_atc_feature.html
2. 'Meet the Press', *NBC*, 16 September 2001, op cit.
3. See the official presentation of the base on *DCMilitary*: http://dcmilitary.com/baseguides/airforce/andrews/partnerunits.html
4. 'PAVE PAWS, Watching North America's Skies, 24 Hours a Day', official site: http://www.pavepaws.org/
See also, on the site of the Federation of American Scientists: http://www.fas.org/spp/military/program/track/pavepaws.htm
For further details: National Security Space Road Map (NSSRM): http://www.wslfweb.org/docs/roadmap/irm/internet/surwarn/cat/html/gbss.htm
and: www.wslfweb.org/docs/roadmap/irm/internet/surwarn/roadmap/surwarn.htm

Contrary to the Pentagon's claims, the military thus knew perfectly well that an unidentified vehicle was headed straight for the capital. Yet the military did not react and Pentagon's anti-missile batteries did not function. Why?

The close-range anti-aircraft defenses at the Pentagon are conceived to destroy missiles that attempt to approach. A missile should normally be unable to pass. As for a big Boeing 757-200, it would have strictly no chance.

Whether an airliner or a missile, an explanation needs to be found. Is the military technology of the United States totally inefficient? Or was it in fact sabotaged?

If it was a missile involved, a hypothesis might be formulated that would explain the absence of reaction from the defense system. Each military aircraft in fact possesses a transponder which is much more sophisticated that those of civilian planes, and notably permit it to declare itself in the eyes of its possessor as *friendly* or *hostile*.[1] This system is indispensable to identify the numerous aircraft over a battlefield and to ensure that only enemy vehicles are destroyed. An antimissile battery will not, for example, react to the passage of a friendly missile. It is not impossible that that was what happened at the Pentagon on 11 September 2001.

To continue defending their version of the attack on 11 September, the military are reduced to denigrating themselves, by making us believe in their own incompetence. And each new step, each new question renders even heavier the role of the army in these events.

The fuse

Strangely, only NORAD is presented under the media's spotlights. The entire responsibility is attributed to it for the air defense system on 11 September 2001. It is thus solely to NORAD that any blame attaches for an eventual dysfunction of these defenses. Yet, this organization, set up by the United States with Canada to protect all of the North American airspace, only executes the decisions taken by the National Military Command Center (NMCC) at the Pentagon.

It is in fact the NMCC and not NORAD that centralizes all information concerning plane hijackings and directs military operations. The regulations that we have already quoted and which are authoritative in the matter of plane hijackings is very precise on this subject. "[*The NMCC* [...]

---

1. See notably the presentation of the AN/APX-100(V) transponder: http://www.globalsecurity.org/military/library/policy/navy/ntsp/apx-100A.htm

constitutes the coordinating authority between the Department of Defense, the FAA and the commanders in the field. [...] *These services, the unified command posts and the US elements of NORAD are responsible for the application of these guidelines as well as any other directive, law or international legislation concerning air piracy (hijacking) or derelict airborne objects.*]"[1] This directive from the chiefs of staff is perfectly integrated by the FAA which makes clear in its own regulations that, "[*Military escort will be requested by the FAA official responsible for hijack situations, who will work in close contact with the National Military Command Center (NMCC)*]"[2]

That morning, the NMCC was wide awake when the Pentagon was hit by a flying apparatus... It was even in a state of maximum alert. For more than half an hour, the procedure for Management of Crisis Situations had been activated and the NMC was the nerve center of all military activities. "*Well, the terrible moment was actually earlier at about 8:40, 8:45 when we realized a plane and then a second plane had hit the World Trade Center. And immediately the crisis management process started up,*" explained the assistant to Defense Secretary, Victoria Clarke. "*A couple of us had gone into the secretary's office, Secretary Rumsfeld's office, to alert him to that, tell him that the crisis management process was starting up. He wanted to make a few phone calls. So a few of us headed across the hallway to an area called the National Military Command Center.*"[3]

It was thus at the NMCC, in the heart of the Pentagon, and not at NORAD, that the actions of 11 September were coordinated. It was to this strategic center that the FAA fed all information concerning the hijacked planes or susceptible of being relevant to them. It was to this nerve center that information came about the flying object heading for the capital. Yet it's NORAD that is presented in the media as the sole body responsible. As for the NMCC, it almost never gets mentioned. It all looks as though NORAD served as the scapegoat, ready to take the blame for an eventual failure of operations on 11 September.

At the NMCC, the highest military authority is the Chairman of the Joint Chiefs of Staff. On September 11, this function was still being carried out by General Henry Shelton. But at the time of these

---

1. 'Aircraft Piracy (Hijacking) and Destruction of Derelict Airborne Objects', op cit.
2. 'Special Military Operations', Order 7610.4J, 3 November 1998, including the modifications of 3 July 2000 and 12 July 2001: http://faa.gov/ATpubs/MIL/Ch7/mil0701.html#7-1-2
3. Interview with Victoria Clarke, *WBZ Boston Saturday*, 15 September 2001: http://www.defenselink.mil/news/Sep2001/t09162001_t0915wbz.html

events, he was en route for Europe, "*somewhere over the Atlantic*", said the armed forces' information service.[1] In his absence, it was thus his deputy, the Vice Chairman of the Joint Chiefs of Staff, who assured the continuity of the defense of the United States. From February 2000, this man was General Richard Myers, of the Air Force, who had been appointed several day's earlier as Chairman in replacement of Henry Shelton. Yet General Myers was not there, either. He even greatly emphasized his absence during the events, declaring that he watched the attacks on television, "*like watching a bad movie*".[2] During the attacks, he was in the Capitol building where he saw a television reporting that a plane had hit the World Trade Center. "*They thought it was a small plane or something like that,*" he explained. He then entered the office of Senator Max Cleland with whom he had an appointment. Then the second tower was attacked. "*Nobody informed us of that,*" Myers said. "*But when we came out, that was obvious. Then, right at that time, somebody said the Pentagon had been hit.*" It was only after the events that the general arrived at the National Military Command Center.

* * *

According to the information released by the army, on 11 September 2001, the only parties responsible were NORAD and its commander-in-chief, General Ralph Eberhart. Along the way, one forgets that the National Military Command Center, in the heart of the Pentagon, was the nerve center of all operations. The armed forces' information service insists on the fact that the outgoing Chairman of the Joint Chiefs of Staff, General Henry Shelton, was "*somewhere over the Atlantic*". And the new Chairman, Richard Myers, claims for his part that he watched the attacks on television. That day, a lot of military officers weren't responsible.

The fact remains that the disappearance of American Airlines flight 77 continues unexplained, as does the firing of a missile at the Pentagon, the insider trading committed before September 11, the collapse of tower n° 7 in New York and the fire in the White House annex.

---

1. 'Myers and Sept. 11: We Hadn't Thought About This', *American Forces Information Service*, Defense Link, Department of Defense, 23 October 2001:
http://www.defenselink.mil/news/Oct2001/n10232001_200110236.html
2. Myers and Sept. 11: We Hadn't Thought About This', op cit.

In order to find what happened to the plane, its crew and its passengers, we are obliged to turn to the military. But their explanations continue to pose problems. To each question raised, they are in an awkward position and have to answer with: technical failure, coordination problems, temporary incapacity, transfer of responsibility, absence of commanders, etc. In the end, the greatest army in the world is obliged to confess that it's also the most incompetent.

EPILOGUE

The lies of the Bush government as to the real nature of the attack committed at the Pentagon constitute a serious blow to American democracy and international law. By manipulating their fellow citizens and the rest of the world, they seek endorsement of their illegitimate decisions. They represent a form of governance, the "reason of State", that the founders of the United States of America wanted to definitively overthrow by establishing a "lawful State" guaranteed by the Constitution and a "Bill of Rights".

Already, American citizens, through petition as well as through their senators and representatives, are demanding the creation of Congressional commissions of inquiry into the September 11 attacks.

As of now, only Congress can elucidate these events and take appropriate sanctions against the civilian and military personalities implicated.

The great people that was capable of forcing the resignation of President Nixon following the Watergate affair, should today draw lessons from this "*Pentagate*", out of a desire for justice and fidelity to the memory of the victims of 11 September 2001 and the war in Afghanistan.

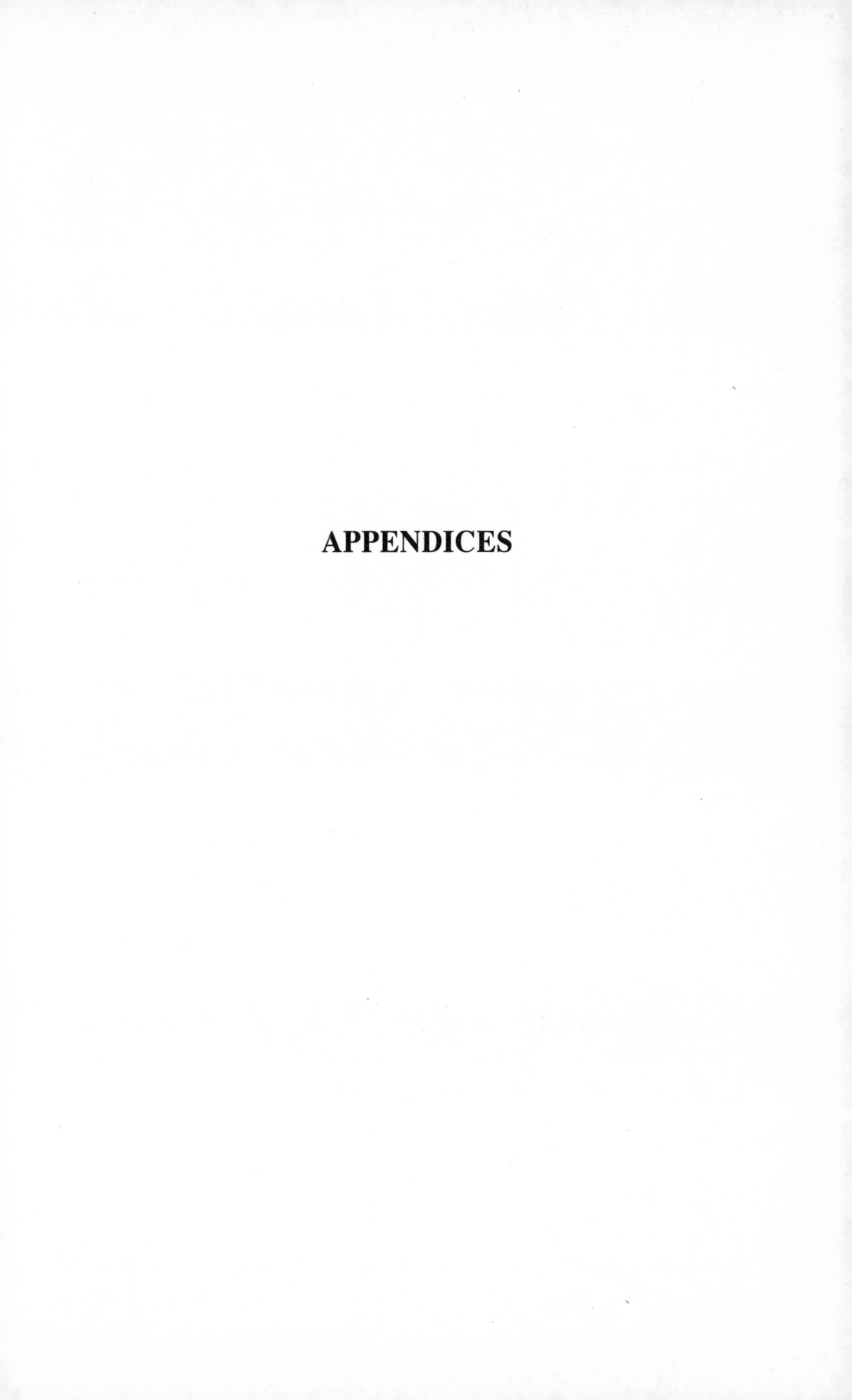

APPENDICES

OPINION ARTICLE
BY CYNTHIA McKINNEY *

"It's important that Bush answer the questions raised by the events of September 11"

12 April 2002

The need for an investigation of the events surrounding September 11 is as obvious as is the need for an investigation of the Enron debacle. Certainly, if the American people deserve answers about what went wrong with Enron and why (and we do), then we deserve to know what went wrong on September 11 and why.

Are we squandering our goodwill around the world with what many believe to be incoherent, warmongering policies that alienate our friends and antagonize our allies? How much of a role does our reliance on imported oil play in the military policies being put forward by the Bush Administration? And what role does the close relationship between the Bush Administration and the oil and defense industries play, if any, in the policies that are currently being pursued by this Administration?

We deserve to know what went wrong on September 11 and why. After all, we hold thorough public inquiries into rail disasters, plane crashes, and even natural disasters in order to understand what happened and to prevent them from happening again or minimizing the tragic effects when they do. Why then does the Administration remain steadfast in its opposition to an investigation into the biggest terrorism attack upon our nation?

News reports from *Der Spiegel* to the *London Observer*, from the *Los Angeles Times* to MSNBC to CNN, indicate that many different warnings were received by the Administration. In addition, it has even been reported that the United States government broke bin Laden's secure communications before September 11. Sadly, the United States government is being sued today by survivors of the Embassy bombings because, from court reports, it appears clear that the US had received prior warnings, but did little to secure and protect the staff at our embassies.

Did the same thing happen to us again?

I am not aware of any evidence showing that President Bush or members of his administration have personally profited from the attacks of 9-11. A complete investigation might reveal that to be the case. For example, it is known that President Bush's father, through the Carlyle Group had – at the time of the attacks – joint business interests with the bin Laden construction company and many defense industry holdings, the stocks of which, have soared since September 11.

On the other hand, what is undeniable is that corporations close to the Administration, have directly benefited from the increased defense spending arising from the aftermath of September 11. The Carlyle Group, DynCorp, and Halliburton certainly stand out as companies close to this Administration. Secretary Rumsfeld maintained in a hearing before Congress that we can afford the new spending, even though the request for more defense spending is the highest increase in twenty years and the Pentagon has lost $2.3 trillion.

All the American people are being asked to make sacrifices. Our young men and women in the military are being asked to risk their lives in our War Against Terrorism while our President's first act was to sign an executive order denying them high deployment overtime pay. The American people are being asked to make sacrifices by bearing massive budget cuts in the social welfare of our country, in the areas of health care, social security, and civil liberties for our enhanced military and security needs arising from the events of September 11; it is imperative that they know fully why we make the sacrifices. If the Secretary of Defense tells us that his new military objectives must be to occupy foreign capital cities and overthrow regimes, then the American people must know why. It should be easy for this Administration to explain fully to the American people in a thorough and methodical way why we are being asked to make these sacrifices and if, indeed, these sacrifices will make us more secure. If the Administration cannot articulate these answers to the American people, then the Congress must.

This is not a time for closed-door meetings and this is not a time for secrecy. America's credibility, both with the world and with her own people, rests upon securing credible answers to these questions. The world is teetering on the brink of conflicts while the Administration's policies are vague, wavering and unclear. Major financial conflicts of interest involving the President, the Attorney General, the Vice President and others in the Administration have been and continue to be exposed.

This is a time for leadership and judgment that is not compromised in any fashion. This is a time for transparency and a thorough investigation.

** Cynthia McKinney is the Congresswoman (Democrat) for the 4th district of Georgia.*
Official Web site: http://www.house.gov/mckinney

OPINION ARTICLE
BY CYNTHIA McKINNEY *

"I was derided by spokespersons for the military-industrial complex as a conspiracy theorist."
16 May 2002

Several weeks ago, I called for a congressional investigation into what warnings the Bush Administration received before the terrorist attacks of September 11, 2001. I was derided by the White House, right wing talk radio, and spokespersons for the military-industrial complex as a conspiracy theorist. Even my patriotism was questioned because I dared to suggest that Congress should conduct a full and complete investigation into the most disastrous intelligence failure in American history. Georgia Senator Zell Miller even went so far as to characterize my call for hearings as "*dangerous, loony and irresponsible.*"

Today's revelations that the administration, and President Bush, were given months of notice that a terrorist attack was a distinct possibility points out the critical need for a full and complete congressional investigation.

It now becomes clear why the Bush Administration has been vigorously opposing congressional hearings. The Bush Administration has been engaged in a conspiracy of silence. If committed and patriotic people had not been pushing for disclosure today's revelations would have been hidden by the White House.

Because I love my country, because I am a patriot, and because the American people deserve the truth, I believe it would be dangerous, loony and irresponsible not to hold full congressional hearings on any warnings the Bush Administration had before the terrorist attacks of September 11, 2001.

Ever since I came to Congress in 1992, there are those who have been trying to silence my voice. I've been told to "*sit down and shut up*" over and over again. Well, I won't sit down and I won't shut up until the full and unvarnished truth is placed before the American people.

DIGIPRESSE INTERVIEW *

Ed Royce: "We are the victims"

Ed Royce was not a witness of the attack that struck the Pentagon. The Republican Congressman from California is nevertheless positive – it was in fact a Boeing 757-200. The proof: he personally knows the victims of the crash, notably the pilot, a former classmate. That's enough for him. The rest is negationism and pro-radical Islamic propaganda.

"*Look what he's done again*," says Ed Royce handing us a transcript of Thierry Meyssan's speech before the Arab League on 8 April 2002. For the Representative of the state of California, the author of *The Big Lie* distorts the facts. He accuses him of playing the game of pro-radical Islamic propaganda. "*I went to Afghanistan, and you know what I heard on the Taliban radio? They said: all that's an American plot to unjustly accuse Osama bin-*

Laden!" And Ed Royce becomes indignant: "*We are the victims.*" This rhetoric stems, according to him, from negationism. To call into question the reality of the attack on the Pentagon is as serious as doubting the existence of concentration camps. "*My father saw Dachau, he showed me the photos* [...] *and yet I heard him fighting against people who claimed the Holocaust never took place or that the Jews provoked it themselves by accusing others.*"

"Lies"

When one questions Ed Royce about the lack of evidence produced by the authorities concerning the crash at the Pentagon, he satisfies himself with a few photos of debris, that are nevertheless unauthenticated as such. It can only be a radical Islamic attack organized with external assistance. "*We know who committed these acts,*" he declares with total assurance. In contrast to Cynthia McKinney, the Democratic Congresswoman from Georgia, Ed Royce sees no interest in calling for a Congressional inquiry. "*What is inexplicable*" is "*this book*", a "*tissue of lies*".

However, the Representative of the state of California evades certain questions. What does he make of the phone call received by the Secret Service at the White House, emanating from anonymous individuals who presented themselves with the identification and transmission codes of the Presidency? This information was reported by the *Washington Post*, the *New York Times* and the *WorldNetDaily*. Ed Royce carefully avoids answering us, pretending to believe this information comes from *The Big Lie*, and concludes that it is fraudulent in nature. They would in fact be American lies, because they have been proffered by the most serious press organs in the country. It's difficult for Ed Royce to admit that in the United States itself, one still can ask questions about the events of 9/11. The possibility of internal complicity is, on the other hand, inconceivable.

According to Congressman Royce, thanks to their institutions, Americans are "*well-protected*" from lobbying attempts. The Constitution and the law shelter politicians from a coup d'etat. He counts enormously on bipartisanship to permit a sort of countervailing power, each party checking the other. Is this theory of the balance of political forces still applicable today? That is not the opinion of Democratic Congresswoman Cynthia McKinney. In these times of war, it seems impossible to exercise any control over the Republican administration, and this is prevented in the name of national unity and the war against terrorism.

Valérie Labrousse

*Interview available on video at the following Internet address:
http://digipressetmp4.teaser.fr/site/page.php?num_art=497&doss=60

Official Web site of Congressman Ed Royce:
http://www.house.gov/royce

DIGIPRESSE INTERVIEW *

Cynthia McKinney: "The conspiracy of silence"

For several days now, nobody makes fun anymore of Cynthia McKinney in the corridors of Congress. Her peers were not mocking the Democratic Congresswoman from George for her colorful attire. Only a few days after the events of 9/11, McKinney was already on the warpath... against the sudden omnipotence of the Bush administration and the restrictions of freedom imposed by the Patriot Act.

"*What did the Bush administration know and when did it learn about it?*" asks Cynthia McKinney. At the time we interviewed her, colleagues, whether Democrats or Republicans, accompanied her interventions before Congress with jeers. Today, with the international press devoting its front pages to the "*mea culpa*" of the White House, the Representative of the state of Georgia is no longer on duty as Congress's anti-patriotic, conspiracy theory crank. Although Cynthia McKinney's words might be more moderate. From 21 September, she has bitterly criticized the process of restricting fundamental civil liberties unleashed by the White House in the name of the war against terrorism. But above all, she asks publicly why no security measures were taken prior to 11 September, when the CIA and the FBI were apparently informed of imminent attacks on American territory.

Tony Blair, Bush's foreign minister

Cynthia McKinney also wonders about the fate of an American intelligence officer detained in Canada, a certain Delmart Vreeland, who is supposed to have tried to warn the Canadian secret services of the attacks yet to come. These are not the fantastical allegations of an "*imposter*", but public statements of a representative of the American people. The Congresswoman's worries are equally those of 12,000 people, mostly American citizens, who signed an online petition demanding an official inquiry into the "peculiarities" of the events (see the interview with Carlos Jacinto). The prime mover behind this petition, Lori Price, has for her part told

Digipresse that she would send a copy of this document to the Congresswoman from Georgia who is intent on voicing the questions of her fellow citizens. In the name of the latter, as early as 25 September she was demanding "*irrefutable proof*" of the culpability of Osama bin Laden and the Taliban government. She has not obtained satisfaction up to this day.

Cynthia McKinney does not hesitate to accuse the Bush administration of having dispatched Tony Blair, "*the real American foreign minister*" on missions instead of Colin Powell, who imprudently promised a report on the events. This obstinacy in demanding a serious investigation has brought down upon her the wrath of Republicans, who see her as anti-patriotic. Now, an investigation into Republican affairs might reveal "*too much information*". And the Democrats, like Thomas Daschle, their Senate leader, won't take the risk, feeling constrained to submit to the consensual view: those against the war are against the United States. "*In a time of national unity,*" McKinney says ironically in an imitation of President Bush, "*we couldn't allow ourselves that* [...] *so let us continue our war against terrorism*". It's what Cynthia McKinney calls "*the conspiracy of silence*".

Who profits from the crime?

Cynthia McKinney also wants explanations about the enormous profits generated by unusual stock market movements several days before 9/11. According to her, the amounts at stake total billions upon billions of dollars. The scandal involves insider trading that would implicate a number of holdings, "*very big players*", big enough to be comparable with national governments. The Congresswoman refers to Unocal, responsible for the oil pipeline project in central Asia. Unocal is said to have landed the deal thanks to support from the powerful Carlyle group. One finds this multinational group again listed as the 11th largest manufacturer of American defense equipment. George Bush senior, a member of the Carlyle group's board of directors, made several official visits to Saudi Arabia between 1998 and 2000. On these occasions, he met with representatives of the bin Laden family.

And what about flight 77 crashing into the Pentagon? If Cynthia McKinney hadn't yet read Thierry Meyssan's book at the time we interviewed her, she had on the other hand learned of a document to which the author of *The Big Lie* also makes reference. James Bamford, investigative journalist, reproduced this document, previous classified "Top Secret", in his book, *Body of Secrets*. In it, one discovers that forty years ago certain members of the

American military leadership had planned and approved the organization of attacks on the national territory. Attributed to the Cuban regime, these "*plane-bombs*" would have justified an American attack against Fidel Castro. "*It that was conceivable forty years ago, why not today?*" asks the Congresswoman.

For Cynthia McKinney, the real questions thus remain: "*Who are the authors of the attacks? Why? How? Who helped them? Who knew? And who permitted this to happen?* [...] *The American people deserve to have the answers.*" Has the Representative from Georgia contributed to breaking a taboo? That's by no means certain, the discordant voice of Cynthia McKinney could well be smothered by the probable security measures following the next attacks, which we are told will be even more savage. But this time, the FBI seems to know.

Valérie Labrousse

*Interview available on video at the following Internet address:
http://digipressetmp4.teaser.fr/site/page.php?num_art=498&doss=60

DIGIPRESSE INTERVIEW *

Carlos Jacinto: "A lot of things to clear up"

Carlos Jacinto, 21 years old, is one of the signatories of the online petition demanding explanations for the events of 11 September. The American Senate will soon receive the document signed by only 12,000 Internet users as of date. The interview he granted to Digipresse was prior to the latest revelations concerning the White House.

A student in political science at the University of Washington, Carlos Jacinto is above all an American citizen who questions the "hidden agenda" of the September 11 attacks. "*There are lot of things to clear up,*" he starts by saying. For example, why did "*Bush grant 43 million dollars in aid to the Taliban for the war against drugs in May, only a few months before the attacks*?" His unanswered questions made him decide to sign a petition asking for an inquiry into the responsibilities and circumstances surrounding the events of 11 September. For Carlos, it's not a matter of making wild accusations or formulating a full-fledged indictment, but of simply posing questions.

Economic interests

The "*problem*" according to him does not revolve around the existence of the plane. He doesn't want to express an opinion about a book he hasn't read. It's more the political and economical aspects of the attacks that interest Carlos Jacinto. He wonders about the legitimacy of the financial transactions, the possibility of insider trading and particularly about the strategy of the company Unocal to win the deal for the construction of a pipeline in Afghanistan. What he has difficulty accepting is the idea "*that the taxpayers have paid to help the Taliban, then paid again to support the war effort*". The silence of the Bush government angers him, as do the silences of the Democratic opposition, and of its representative in the Senate, Tom Daschle. Without formulating clearly the word "*plot*", Jacinto ventures as far as saying that the events of "*Nine Eleven*" are closely linked to economic interests. "*The bankruptcy of the company Enron has something to do with all these stories.*"

"A just war"

An American citizen, Carlos Jacinto was, like many of his fellow countrymen, in favor of the war in Afghanistan. "*This war was just because we had deliver these people from the extremists, and after all, we were responding to an attack on American unlike any other since Pearl Harbor!*" But like a number of other American citizens as well, he does not wish to see his country bog down in wars that remind him of Vietnam. "*Before sending our troops throughout the world, we have to know why and justify it, organize it. And I don't see any planning!*"

A petition for an inquiry

The online petition signed by Carlos Jacinto and 12,000 other Internet users, was drawn up by Lori Price, editor and webmistress of Falloutshelternews.com and Legitgov.org. These two sites gather much information about the attacks in the United States. What are questions being raised by Lori Price?

In a general way, she dwelt on the financial transactions that took place just before the attacks. These transactions, principally those involving the United Airlines company, according to an article in the *San Francisco Chronicle*, are said to have permitted anonymous investors to make enormous profits by counting on the closure of the stock exchange during the four days following the crash, and betting on the fall in share prices. Indeed, between 6 and 10 September speculations on a drop in prices permitted the purchase of 4,744 sale options on United Airlines shares against only 395 buy options. The same scenario took place with American Airlines on 10 September (4,516 sales options against 748 buy options). Lastly, Lori Price also wonders about the role of the Carlyle group. This powerful multinational is said to have backed Unocal in its bid for a contract estimated to be worth two billion dollars, for the construction of a pipeline across Afghanistan.

Lori Price's online petition has received for the moment 12,615 signatures. "*I would like to submit it to the Senate and the media when have reached 20,000 signatures.*" The list of unresolved mysteries on "9/11" is a long one. Like that of the profits reaped. The petition, which has been posted on the Net for several months now, enumerates twelve of these mysteries. Number 11 has since taken on a particular resonance. It involves "*the hypothesis that George Bush was warned of the attacks*".

Valérie Labrousse

*Interview available on video at the following Internet address:
http://digipressetmp4.teaser.fr/site/page.php?num_art=496&doss=60

Web sites:
http://www.petitiononline.com/11601TFS/petition.html
http://falloutshelternews.com/
http://www.legitgov.org
http://www.hereinreality.com/insidertrading.html

DIGIPRESSE INTERVIEW *

Mike Walter: "Neither missile nor bomb, an American Airlines plane"

Mike Walters is a journalist for the daily newspaper, *USA Today*. His testimony is crucial because he says he saw it all: the airplane, the trajectory, the impact and the debris.

On the morning of 11 September, Mike Walter was on the Colombia Pike, going in the opposite direction to Steve Riskus. The Pentagon was a few hundred yards on his right when he saw an American Airlines plane pass over him on the left. The plane was headed in the opposite direction to the Pentagon, but he then saw it turn "*fairly slowly*". Next, once the turn was carried out, according to him the plane accelerated, crossed his route and plunged directly at the Pentagon.

Mike Walters is a crucial witness because he describes all of the phases of the catastrophe: the trajectory, its relatively slow speed at the start, its final acceleration and the impact. He also says he saw the American Airlines logo when the vehicle turned towards the Pentagon. He had plenty of time to notice that the plane was low and that it hadn't deployed its landing gear. His statement confirms the other testimonies: the plane hit a lamppost, it entered straight into the building and it did not hit the ground before impact. Traffic was dense, so he was driving slowly, the place where he was had a particularly clear view. His visibility was perfect, in contrast to that of Steve Riskus.

"Disintegration": an ambiguous term

His testimony is much better founded. He says in fact that he stopped and got out of the car because he "*knew that this would be the subject he'd be covering that day*". He was thus able to see pieces of the plane. According to him, if the explosion didn't cause damage to the nearby trees and cars, it was because the violence of the impact was propagated upwards rather than in a horizontal fashion. The airplane, he says, continued on its course inside the Pentagon, but the wings did not enter the building. They were folded back.[1] According to Mike Walter, the explosion was such that the plane disintegrated. Not in the sense that it had disappeared, because this term is ambiguous, but in such a way that it parts were reduced to small pieces disseminated all around. He claims to have seen men gathering the debris and placing it in bags bearing the inscription "*evidence*".

Finally, he explained about the first testimony that he gave to CNN in which he declared, "*it was like a cruise missile with wings*". In reality, he had resorted to using a metaphor because for him, that day, this commercial jet "*was like a missile or a bomb since it was used to kill people*". Mike Walter loses his temper slightly when one tries to put to the test what he saw. "*It wasn't a missile, it wasn't a bomb, it was an airliner from American Airlines and I saw it plunge into the Pentagon.*"

Mike Walter is convinced and convincing. He took the trouble of returning to the scene with us and showing us several times the trajectory of the plane. He pointed out to us the hill where the reporters stood after the tragedy to watch the rescue

---

1. On 21 March 2002, on LCI (French TV news), Mike Walter had another version of the facts: "I saw the jet crash into the building. It was folded like an accordion. There was an explosion, a ball of fire. I got out of my car. I moved forward. There was debris on the ground. I saw it with my own eyes. I can't believe that one can write a book claiming otherwise. There is no doubt in my mind that a plane plunged into the Pentagon. I saw it."

effort. He also indicated on which lawn the wounded were evacuated and mimed the impact with his hands... The sole fly in the ointment is that Mike Walter is the only witness in our investigation to have mentioned seeing the debris. Was that because of his particular position during the impact, further to the southwest of the Pentagon where the crash happened?

Patriotism versus freedom of the press

Beyond the controversy raised by Thierry Meyssan's thesis, we profited from Mike Walter's status as a journalist to ask him about the consequences of the Patriot Act for the freedom of the American press. The restrictions of this law took effect on 11 September and are the subject of a report edited by the Reporters Committee for Freedom of the Press (RCFP) entitled "*How the War Against Terrorism Hinders Access to Information and the Public's Right to Information*". The document notably evokes the difficulties encountered by reporters in Afghanistan, forbidden by the military to travel in strategic zones. Mike Walter did not deny the existence of these obstacles, but according to him this was nothing new, transparency not being – by its essence – a strongpoint of the military. However, he could not imagine the possibility of a plot or any sort of responsibility of military leaders or the American government in the attacks of 11 September. If it that had been the case, the scandal would already have erupted. Because according to him "*nobody can keep a secret in this country, and especially not the government or the military*".

Valérie Labrousse

*Interview available on video at the following Internet address:
http://digipressetmp4.teaser.fr/site/page.php?num_art=492&doss=60

The site of the RCFP:
http://www.rcfp.org/homefrontconfidential/

DIGIPRESSE INTERVIEW *

Richard Benedetto: "That plane is going to crash into the Pentagon!"

The testimony of Richard Benedetto, like Mike Walter a journalist for the daily newspaper, *USA Today*, mentions in detail the last moments of flight AA77. Some of his statements, however, contradict those in other testimonies.

At the time of the tragedy, Richard Benedetto was also on Colombia Pike, en route to his office. He was not far from Steve Riskus and James Ryan, the other witnesses, when the Pentagon appeared on his left. He then distinctly saw an American Airlines plane pass over him to the left, and noticed that it was headed in a direction opposed to Reagan International Airport. The aircraft was flying very low, its landing gear still tucked inside. Right away, he thought that it "*seemed to be hea-*

ding toward the Pentagon". He saw the aircraft accelerate and speed straight at the building. But, like James Ryan, he was unable to see the impact because the hill obstructed his view. However, as James Ryan did, he described the same ball of fire, the same dull noise at impact and the same black smoke rising above the building.

A question of point of view

The testimony of Richard Benedetto corroborates the stories of other witnesses (the AA logo on the tail, the lamppost hit by the plane) with some slight variations, however. He did not see the plain waggle its wings as James Ryan said, and neither did he see the debris evoked by Mike Walter, nor could he make out the plane after the tragedy. "*The smoke was too black and thick to be able to see anything at all.*" It is particularly difficult to judge the trajectory of the Boeing he describes because if the Pentagon is on his left, one does not see very well how the plane could have come from behind him on the left (James Ryan also claims this), since Mike Walter, who saw the Pentagon to his right, also perceived flight 77 coming from the left and then performing its turn. This difference in trajectory is, however; difficult to appreciate, because the route along Colombia Pike turns several times before passing in front of the Pentagon, and if for Steve Riskus the plane cut across the road, it is possible that for Richard Benedetto it was following it.

Lastly, the trajectory described by Mike Walter was the result of guesswork. It was not a reconstruction and it is difficult to say if the distance at which the plane made his turn coincided with the place where, from the other side of the road, Richard Benedetto saw it.

Valérie Labrousse

*Interview available on video at the following Internet address:
http://digipressetmp4.teaser.fr/site/page.php?num_art=491&doss=60

DIGIPRESSE INTERVIEW *

Steve Riskus: "Like in a cartoon"

Steve Riskus, 24 years old is a "hotliner" in the computer industry. He was present during the crash at the Pentagon, where he was the author of the very first photos, right after the impact. He later published them on his Web site *Youthenrage.com*, for which on 10 September he registered a new domain name, *criticalthrash.com*.

On 11 September, towards 9 am, Steve Riskus, 24 year old computer hotliner, was taking Colombia Pike on his way to see a friend. The Pentagon was a few hundred yards away on the left. Suddenly on the right, he saw an airplane cross his path and head directly for the Pentagon. He says he saw everything: the distinctive signs of an American Airlines jetliner, and the blue and red line along the vehicle. He noticed that the aircraft was flying very low, "*at treetops level*", that it was going very fast and that the landing gear had not been deployed. He saw the plane decapitate a highway lamppost and right after hit the wall of the building without touching the ground. "*Like in a cartoon, it exploded immediately, there were flames and smoke, I could not see if the wings had entered the wall*". He then stopped his car on Colombia Pike, where traffic became immediately blocked due to the shock of the explosion and resulting panic. On the side of the road, he took some pictures with his digital camera. After a few moments, still deeply shocked, he got back into his car and drove aimlessly around the Pentagon, but soon the rescue vehicles, the military and the police blocked off the crash scene. He then went to visit a friend and put his photos online on his site *Youthenrage.com.*

The testimony of Steve Riskus is clear and precise. He has no doubts about the nature of the flying vehicle he saw pass before his eyes and hit the Pentagon. However, his visibility at the time was reduced, he says himself, by the trees along the road, and doubtless he had very little time, perhaps two seconds, in which to glimpse the aircraft. In that case, did he have time to see all these details, to notice that not only was it in fact a plane, but also one belonging to American Airlines, to see the eagle between the two letters AA, and to understand that it did not have the landing gear deployed? Steve Riskus had just heard about the attacks at the WTC. Did he interpret what he saw in light of that context? Several elements in his testimony tend in any case to contradict the official thesis. According to him, the aircraft entered the building straight on and not at an angle of 45°. Next, it did not strike the ground before exploding against the building. Lastly, Steve Riskus made it clear that he had not seen debris and had stood less than 200 yards from the place of the crash long enough to take many snapshots in which there does not appear any element permitting one to recognize an airplane.

The case of Steve Riskus is particular. This skateboarding fan created a Web site devoted to his favorite sport in October 2000. Now, on 10 September 2001, the eve of the crash, he registered a new domain name, *Criticalthrash.com.* This tag makes one pause, as does the date. Steve Riskus said he thought the new name was more "cutting edge" and had copied it from an expression used by cycling fans, *bycyclethrash*, and registered the name on 10 September because "*everybody did something on that day, I registered this name, it's pure chance*". Initially, he published the photos under both domain names. That very day he placed a link on his homepage, but later decided to suppress it. Only informed people can effectively go to that page by tapping a very exact precise address that is not accessible otherwise. Why? "*Because I didn't want to mix everything up. My Web site has nothing to do with this story. I told people they could see my pictures by typing this address.*" However, if Steve Riskus's reticence about directly posting photos on his site which have nothing to do with its subject is understandable, a few months later, he added to his page about the crash a list of witnesses.

In the meantime, Steve Riskus received e-mails, certain of which alluded the deposit date of his domain name, Criticalthrash.com. "*Even my friends asked me for explanations.*" Then he heard about Thierry Meyssan's book, and was solicited by a Web surfer seeking information. In some discussion forums, the case of Steve Riskus and his *Criticalthrash* appeared "suspect". To be sure, he registered this new name on 10 September. However, his site existed previously under the name *Youthenrage.com*. The registrations were carried out in an open fashion, his surname appears on the registry server. He does not know at what point the registration of *Criticalthrash* became effective. But if one considers that this question only makes sense from the moment one begins to question his motives, one supposes that for him it wasn't very important to know that because in any case his site was already accessible. What he doesn't understand, six months after the crash, is why the press has not used his photos which he offered free of charge and the most immediate ones taken of the event. Another question also remains: in this case, why hasn't the FBI, which claims to have gathered all the evidence in its investigation of the attack, thought it worthwhile to make use of these photos.

A person "with good intentions"

One day he received a strange phone call from France. A person who said he had "*good intentions*" and of whom Steve "*doesn't remember the name any more*" warned him against Thierry Meyssan, who he said was manipulated by the CIA. It's a curious attitude to take the trouble of telephoning from France to warn someone who is not, after all, extremely threatened. Steve Riskus does not seem excessively troubled by the French controversy or by the possibility of an American manipulation being responsible for the attacks on 11 September. The e-mails come, he's used to Internet and responds to everyone but does not become interested in the identity of his correspondents. Had he received an e-mail or a call from Thierry Meyssan or someone from the Réseau Voltaire? He doesn't recall, doesn't think that happened, but what he does know is that he's "*never refused to answer whoever it may be*". That is not what Thierry Meyssan told us, claiming that one of his collaborators talked on the telephone with Riskus, and that the latter hung up in the middle of the conversation.

Valérie Labrousse

* Interview available on video at the following Internet address:
http://digipressetmp4.teaser.fr/site/page.php?num_art=490&doss=60

http://criticalthrash.com/terror/

DIGIPRESSE INTERVIEW *

James Ryan: "It was a nightmare"

James Ryan had not talked previously to the media. He contacted Digipresse after having watched the interview with Thierry Meyssan on the news stream of Yahoo!/Digipresse shortly after the release of *The Big Lie* in France. Meyssan's comments were shocking for this former military officer, but not as shocking as the terrible spectacle of the crash of flight AA77.

James Ryan, 27 years old, works in sales for a computer company and is a former press attaché for the US Navy. That day, he had to go see a mechanic whose shop was on Colombia Pike which runs past the Pentagon. He heard a plane pass over but did not pay real attention to it because there were planes flying over regularly in that area. However, he then noticed a strange noise that he interpreted as being that of the engines being suddenly cut off. He therefore raised his eyes and saw an aircraft at very low altitude that he immediately identified, he says, as an Boeing belonging to American Airlines. He made it clear that he saw the company's logo, that the aircraft was silver in color, and he also says he could distinguish the windows. He became all at once worried because he noticed that the plane was not on a normal trajectory since it wasn't headed towards Reagan International Airport, and above all because it appeared to him that the vehicle was in its landing phase, although neither the wing flaps nor the landing gear had been activated. The plane flew over his car. At that instant he saw it bank its wings as if it was gliding and had just "*avoided the radio tower*" in trying to stabilize itself . The next moment, the plane accelerated powerfully and sped straight ahead in the direction of the west wing of the Pentagon. James Ryan could not see the impact because in that place the ground rose above the road level, but he followed the aircraft as it disappeared behind the trees, then he heard a dull noise and saw an orange ball of fire rising in the sky, followed by thick black smoke. He's certain that it was the aircraft that he saw passing at low altitude. "*A few instants before, the Pentagon was intact and then the plane did not reappear after the crash.*"

Emotional but convinced

On certain points, James Ryan gives the same details as other witnesses. It was an American Airlines aircraft whose tail logo he recognized. He is even more precise in saying that he could see the windows. Very emotional, he admits that he still has nightmares and that he will remember that plane his entire life. He also took photos after the crash, including one of a member of the Navy, looked dazed and in a state of shock.

James Ryan's fragility, however, does not prevent a certain determination when he mimes the plane. And there, what is described could cause some confusion. His very sudden gesture could indeed evoke more the final approach of a missile rather than that of a civilian jet. Since his manner of testifying is indeed extremely subjective and emotional, no objective conclusion can be reasonably drawn here. But his testimony does differ from the others. He is the only person to speak of a peculiar noise equivalent to that an engine losing speed, and the one to have seen the plane pitch as it accelerated.

James Ryan did not wish to return to the scene of the crime. He still has nightmares and remembers "*all the details of that plane*". His eyes blur with tears as he tells that a few instants after the tragedy he saw in the sky, above the black smoke rising from the Pentagon, two eagles soaring over the dramatic scene. A couple of birds who are well-known in the area, it seems. "*It was like a sign that we were going to find our strength again, like the Phoenix being reborn from its ashes.*"

Valérie Labrousse

* Interview available on video at the following Internet address:
http://digipressetmp4.teaser.fr/site/page.php?num_art=488&doss=60

DIGIPRESSE INTERVIEW *

Ed Plaugher: Memory in Reverse

Ed Plaugher, the Arlington fire chief, was with his men on the scene of the attack to take part alongside the Federal teams in rescue efforts and fighting the fire that propagated itself within the Pentagon for several days.

Ed Plaugher almost laughs as he affirms: "*I can assure you that it was a plane*". Talkative, the fire chief of Arlington county enumerates an exhaustive list of the debris he says he saw at the site of the impact: "*wings, the fuselage, seats, engines, landing gear, and the black box*". On 12 September, however, he told journalists at a briefing in the Pentagon that there was only "*small pieces of plane, and above all, no fuselage and no important debris*".

His uncertain tone almost resembles the embarrassment he betrayed when he almost refused to testify at that same press conference, where they asked him what he thought about the origin of the debris found on the highway in front of the Pentagon. At the he indicated that had seen nothing and preferred that journalists address themselves directly to eyewitnesses. Ed Plaugher has thus recovered his memory. But how could he have seen the seats forty minutes after the explosion if the plane had, as the authorities claim, literally disintegrated? In his testimony for Digipresse, the fire chief also explains about the use of water in a kerosene fire. Explanations that at first sight seem plausible according the press attaché of the Paris fire department. Water, Ed Plaugher tells us, is not used to fight a kerosene fire "*as long as the fuel is liquid, but once it's consumed with the objects, once it evaporates, then you can use it*". To be sure, but as Ed Plaugher himself says: water was utilized as the "*first agent*", something which, according to the French fire department official, seems doubtful unless the water was being used away from the heart of the blaze.

Another mystery is that, although Ed Plaugher claims to have seen them, according to official sources the plane's black boxes were found only on 14 September "*at the very spot where the plane crashed into the Pentagon*". The same day, Dick Bridges, another fire officer, said that they were damaged but the FBI thought they might be able to extract data from them. Shortly after, the FBI claimed that they provided no usable data. Six months after the attacks, however, the FBI issued a statement protesting against Thierry Meyssan's work and pointing to the existence as a crucial element of evidence the data from these black boxes...

Contradictions are thus frequent among the pieces of information given to the public over many months. Thus, at the beginning, there were no major pieces of debris, because the impact and fire had made everything disappear.

Confidential evidence

The FBI refused to meet with us, but nevertheless agreed to answer some questions by telephone. Its representative claimed, while releasing an official statement concerning Thierry Meyssan's book, that the FBI already had in its possession all the evidence necessary to prove the existence of a plane. So today there do in fact exist traces of flight 77 with debris authenticated by a "*serial number of the airline company*". However, when asked why these elements were not shown to the press and the public, thus silencing the detractors of the official thesis, the FBI spokesman, Fred Murnay declared that the investigation "*isn't over*" and that consequently, evidence would remain confidential.

Yet, according the FBI's Web site, since 26 September, the investigation had been taken over by the DoD, the American Defense ministry. Questioned on this subject, Fred Murnay denied it. Lost in the Kafkaesque meanderings of the Federal administration, we ended by obtaining the name of the prosecutor in charge of the investigation. This was prosecutor McNulty, attached to the department for Arlington county where the Pentagon is located. He refused to speak with us and his press attaché concluded a conversation with the words: "*this investigation is not close to being ended*". Alright, but how long will it take? "*No doubt, years.*" One can thus wonder what the FBI discovered in its investigation and its harvest of evidence, because if the elements have "all been gathered together", as Fred Murnay claims, why haven't public proceedings started?

Valérie Labrousse

* Interview available on video at the following Internet address:
http://digipressetmp4.teaser.fr/site/page.php?num_art=487&doss=60

NORAD'S RESPONSE TIMES

(15 September 2001)

NORTH AMERICAN AEROSPACE DEFENSE COMMAND

Directorate of Public Affairs, Headquarters, North American Aerospace Defense Command & US Space Command,
250 S. Peterson Blvd, Suite 116, Peterson AFB, Colorado Springs, Colo. 80914-3190 Phone (719) 554-6889 DSN 692-6889
NORAD and US Space Command website address: http://www.peterson.af.mil/norad or http://www.peterson.af.mil/usspacecom

NORAD'S Response Times

PETERSON AFB, Colo. --The following timelines show NORAD's response to the airliner hijackings on September 11, 2001.

* All times are Eastern Daylight Time; NEADS = North East Air Defense Sector, NORAD
** Scramble = Order to get an aircraft airborne as soon as possible
***Estimated = loss of radar contact
**** Flight times are calculated at 9 miles per minute or .9 Mach
***** The FAA and NEADS established a line of open communication discussing AA Flt 77 and UA Flt 93

American Airlines Flight 11 – Boston enroute to Los Angeles

FAA Notification to NEADS		0840*
Fighter Scramble Order *(Otis Air National Guard Base, Falmouth, Mass. Two F-15s)*	0846**	
Fighters Airborne		0852
Airline Impact Time (World Trade Center 1)		0846 *(estimated)****
Fighter Time/Distance from Airline Impact Location		Aircraft not airborne/153 miles

United Airlines Flight 175 – Boston enroute to Los Angeles

FAA Notification to NEADS		0843
Fighter Scramble Order *(Otis ANGB, Falmouth, Mass. Same 2 F-15s as Flight 11)*	0846	
Fighters Airborne		0852
Airline Impact Time (World Trade Center 2)		0902 *(estimated)*
Fighter Time/Distance from Airline Impact Location		approx 8 min****/71 miles

American Flight 77 –Dulles enroute to Los Angeles

FAA Notification to NEADS		0924
Fighter Scramble Order *(Langley AFB, Hampton, Va. 2 F-16s)*	0924	
Fighters Airborne		0930
Airline Impact Time (Pentagon)		0937*(estimated)*
Fighter Time/Distance from Airline Impact Location		approx 12 min/105 miles

United Flight 93 – Newark to San Francisco

FAA Notification to NEADS		N/A *****
Fighter Scramble Order *(Langley F-16s already airborne for AA Flt 77)*		
Fighters Airborne *(Langley F-16 CAP remains in place to protect DC)*		
Airline Impact Time (Pennsylvania)		1003 *(estimated)*
Fighter Time/Distance from Airline Impact Location	*(from DC F-16 CAP)*	approx 11 min/100 miles

LECTURE BY THIERRY MEYSSAN, AS GUEST SPEAKER OF THE ARAB LEAGUE

"Who's Behind the September 11 Attacks?"
8 April 2002

We reproduce here below a translation of the text of a lecture given by Thierry Meyssan on 8 April 2002 at the Zayed Center in Abu Dhabi (United Arab Emirates), as a guest of the Arab League and in the presence of the diplomatic corps and the international press.

In the first minutes following the first attack on the World Trade Center, officials suggested to the media that the person behind the attacks was Osama bin Laden, the epitome of Muslim fanaticism. Not long after, the recently appointed director of the FBI, Robert Mueller III, designated nineteen kamikazes by name and mobilized all the means at the disposal of his agency to track down their accomplices. The FBI thus never undertook any investigation but, instead, organized a manhunt, which, in the eyes much of the United States public, quickly took on the appearance of an Arab hunt. This reached such a pitch that people were incited to attack – even kill – Arabs whom they naively considered collectively responsible for the attacks.

There was no investigation by Congress, which, at the request of the White House, renounced exercising its constitutional role, supposedly in order not to adversely affect national security. Nor was there investigation by any media representatives, who had been summoned to the White House and prevailed upon to abstain from following up any leads lest such inquiries also adversely affect national security.

If we analyze the attacks of September the eleventh, we notice first off that there was much more to them than the official version acknowledges.

1. We know about only four planes, whereas at one point it was a question of eleven planes. Further, an examination of the insider-trading conducted in relation to the attacks shows put-option speculative trading in the stock of three airline companies: American Airlines, United Airlines and KLM Royal Dutch Airlines.

2. The official version does not include the attack on the White House annex, the Old Executive Office Building (called the "Eisenhower Building"). Yet, on the morning of the eleventh, ABC television broadcast, live, pictures of a fire ravaging the presidential services building.

3. Neither does the official version take into account the collapse of a third building in Manhattan World Trade Center complex, independently of the twin towers. This third building was not hit by a plane. However, it, too, was ravaged by a fire before collapsing for an unknown reason. This building contained the world's biggest secret CIA operations base, where the Agency engaged in economic intelligence gathering that the military-industrial lobby considered a waste of resources that should have been devoted to strategic intelligence gathering.

If we look closely at the attack against the Pentagon, we notice that the official version amounts to an enormous lie. According to the Defense Department, a Boeing 757, all trace of which had been lost somewhere over Ohio, flew some 500 kilometers (300 miles) without being noticed. It supposedly entered Pentagon air space and descended on to the lawn surrounding the heliport, bounced off the lawn, broke a wing in collision with an electric transformer station, hit the façade at the level of the ground floor and first story, and was totally consumed by fire, leaving no other traces than two dysfunctional black boxes and pieces of passengers' bodies.

It is obviously impossible that a Boeing 757 could, for some 500 kilometers, escape detection by civil and military radar, by fighter-bomber planes sent in pursuit of it and by observation satellites that had just been activated.

It is also obviously impossible that a Boeing 757 could enter the Pentagon's air space without being destroyed by one or more of the five missile batteries protecting the building.

When one examines the photographs of the façade, taken in the minutes following the attack (even before the Arlington civilian fire fighters had time to deploy), one sees no trace of the right wing on fire in front of the façade, nor any hole in the façade into which the plane could have been swallowed up.

Apparently without the least fear of laying itself open to ridicule, the Defense Department declared that the jet engines, made out of tempered steel, had disintegrated under the shock of the impact - without damaging the façade. The aluminum of the fuselage is claimed to have combusted at more than 2,500° Celsius [4,500° F] within the building and to have been transformed into gas, but the bodies of the passengers which it contained were so little burned that they were later identified from their finger prints.

Responding to journalists during a press conference at the Pentagon, the fire chief claimed that "*no voluminous debris from the aircraft*" had remained, "*nor any piece of the fuselage, nor anything of that sort*". He declared that neither he nor his men knew what had become of the aircraft.

Close examination of the official photographs of the scene of the attack, taken and published by the Defense Department, shows that no part of the Pentagon bears any mark of an impact that could be attributed to the crash of a Boeing 757.

One must acknowledge the evidence: it is impossible that the attack against the Pentagon on September 11, killing 125 persons, was carried out by a jet airliner.

The scene of the attack was thoroughly disturbed on the following day by the immediate launch of new construction work, with the result that many of the elements necessary to reconstruct what had happened are missing. The elements that do remain, however, converge in a single hypothesis that it is not possible to prove with certainty.

An air traffic controller from Washington has testified seeing on radar an object flying at about 800 kilometers per hour, moving initially toward the White House, then turning sharply toward the Pentagon, where it seemed to crash. The air traffic controller has testified that the characteristics of the flight were such that it could only have been a military projectile.

Several hundred witnesses have claimed that they head "*a shrill noise like the noise of a fighter-bomber*", but nothing like the noise of a civilian aircraft.

Eye-witnesses have said that they saw "*something like a cruise missile with wings*" or a small flying object "*like a plane carrying eight or twelve persons*".

The flying object penetrated the building without causing major damage to the façade. It crossed several of the building rings of the Pentagon, creating in each wall it pierced a progressively bigger hole. The final hole, perfectly circular, measured about one meter eighty in diameter. When traversing the first ring of the Pentagon, the object set off a fire, as gigantic as it was sudden. Huge flames burst from the building licking the façades, then they shrank back just as fast, leaving behind a cloud of black soot. The fire spread through a part of the first ring and along two perpendicular corridors. It was so sudden that the fire protection system could not react.

All these testimonies and observations correspond to the effects of an AGM [air to ground missile]-86C of the third (most recent) generation of CALCM [conventional air launched cruise missile[1]], equipped with depleted uranium warheads and guided by GPS [global positioning system]. This type of missile, seen from the side, would easily remind one of a small civilian airplane, but it is not a plane. It produces a shrill whistle comparable to that of a fighter-bomber, can be guided with enough accuracy to be directed through a window, can pierce the most resistant armor and can set off a fire – independent of its piercing effect – that will generate heat of over 2,000° Celsius [3,600° F].

This type of missile was developed jointly by the Navy and the Air Force and is fired from a plane. The missile used against the Pentagon destroyed the part of the building where the new Supreme Naval Command Center was being installed. Following the attack, the Navy Chief of Staff, Admiral Vern Walters, failed to show up in the crisis room of the National Military Joint Intelligence Center when the other members of the Joint Chiefs of Staff reported there. Instead, he abruptly left the Pentagon.

Who, then, could have fired such a missile on the Pentagon? The answer was given by the off-the-record revelations of Ari Fleischer, the White House spokesman, and by Karl Rove, senior advisor to the president, to journalists from the New York Times and the Washington Post. Eighteen days later, these men discounted the veracity of the information they had given the journalists, claiming that they had been speaking under the stress of great emotion.

---

1. See picture at: http://www.fas.org/man/dod-101/sys/smart/agm-86c.htm

According to those close to George W. Bush, in the course of the morning, the Secret Service received a telephone call from those behind the attacks, apparently in order to make demands. To give credence to their demands, the masterminds revealed the secret codes giving access to the secure telephone lines available to the president for secure communication with the various intelligence agencies and services as well as for access to the nuclear arsenal. In fact, only a very few persons with the highest security clearances, in the top ranks of the government, could have had these codes. It follows that at least one of the persons behind the attacks of September 11 has a top government post, either civilian or military.

To give credence to the fable of Islamic terrorists, the United States authorities invented kamikazes.

Although it would have been possible for a well organized group of persons to bring fire arms into commercial air liners, the kamikazes apparently used cardboard cutters as their only weapons. They are said to have learned to pilot Boeing 757s and 767s in the space of several hours of simulator training, becoming better pilots than professionals. This mastery allowed them to carry out complex in-flight approach maneuvers.

The Justice Department has never explained how it established the list of the kamikazes. The airline companies have furnished the exact number of passengers in each plane, and the passenger lists, incomplete, do not mention the persons who boarded at the last minute. In checking the these lists, one notices that names of the kamikazes are not on them and that only three passengers are not identified for flight 11 and only two for flight 93. It is thus impossible that 19 kamikazes boarded. Further, several of those listed as kamikazes have turned up, alive. The FBI nonetheless maintains that the hijackers have all been definitively identified and that complementary information such as birth dates makes it improbable that they could be confused with persons of the same name. For those who might doubt this, the FBI has a ridiculous proof: whereas the planes burned and the twin towers collapsed, the passport of Mohammed Atta was miraculously found intact on the smoking ruins of the World Trade Center.

The existence of hijackers, whether these or others, is confirmed by telephone calls made by several passengers to members of their families. Unfortunately, these conversations are known to us only by hearsay and have not been published, even in the case of those that were recorded. Thus, it has been impossible to verify that they were actually made from a particular cell phone of from a telephone on board. Here, too, we are asked to take the FBI at its word.

Further, it was not indispensable to have hijackers to carry out the attacks. The Global Hawk technology, developed by the Air Force, makes it possible to take control of a commercial airliner regardless of the intentions of its pilot(s) and to direct it by remote control.

There remains the case of Osama bin Laden. If it is generally admitted that he was a CIA agent or collaborator during the war against the Soviet Union in Afghanistan, the current version of events claims that he turned coat and became public enemy number one of the United States. This story does not bear up under scrutiny either. The French daily le Figaro revealed that last July, Osama bin Laden was a patient at the American hospital in Dubai, where he was visited by the head of CIA regional office. CBS television in the United States has revealed that, on September 10, Osama bin Laden was undergoing dialysis at the Rawalpindi military hospital, under the protection of the Pakistani army. And the renown French journalist Michel Peyrard, who was a prisoner of the Taliban, has recounted how, last November, Osama bin Laden was living openly in Jalalabad while the United States was bombing other regions of the country. It is difficult to believe that the greatest army in the world, come to Afghanistan to arrest him, was unable to do so, while the mollah Omar was able to escape from United States military force on a moped.

In view of the elements that I have just presented, it appears that the attacks of September can not be attributed to foreign terrorists from the Arab-Muslim world – even if some of those involved might have been Muslim – but to United States terrorists.

The day after the attacks of September 11, United Nations Security Council Resolution 1368 acknowledged "*the inherent right of individual or collective self-defense in accordance with the Charter*", calling on "*all States to work together urgently to bring to justice the perpetrators, organizers and sponsors of these terrorist attacks and stresses that those responsible for aiding, supporting or harboring the perpetrators, organizers and sponsors of these acts will be held accountable*".

If one wishes to heed the call of the Security Council, to enforce Resolution 1368 and to punish those who really are guilty, the only way to accurately identify the guilty parties is to set up a commission of inquiry whose independence and objectivity are guaranteed by the United Nations. This would also be the only way to preserve international peace. In the meantime, Your Highness, Excellencies, Ladies and Gentlemen, the foreign military interventions of the United States of America are devoid of any basis in international law, whether it be their recent intervention in Afghanistan or their announced interventions in Iran, Iraq and in numerous other countries.

Web site of the Zayed Center:
http://www.zccf.org.ae

Arab version of lecture:
http://www.zccf.org.ae/LECTURES/A2_lectures/201.htm

Spanish version:
http://www.reseauvoltaire.net/actu/ligue-arabe_es.htm

TABLE OF CONTENTS

Interview with Ed Plaugher: Memory in Reverse.

NORAD's Response Times.

Lecture by Thierry Meyssan, as guest speaker of the Arab League: "Who's Behind the September 11 Attacks?"